CompTIA Linux+ (Plus) Certification The Ultimate Study Guide to Ace the Exam

Table of Contents

Table of Contents

Introduction

Chapter 1: Introduction to Linux

What is Linux?

What is an Operating System?

How was Linux Developed?

Linux and GNU System

Linux Distributions:

Linux Implementations:

Linux Desktop:

Linux Server:

Mobile Linux:

Embedded Linux:

Linux and Virtualization:

Practice Questions and Answers

Chapter 2: Installing Linux

System Requirements:

Choosing a Distribution:

Installation Media:

Installation Process:

Troubleshooting:

Practice Questions and Answers

Chapter 3: The Linux Shell

Basic Terminal Editing:

Auto-Completion:

Getting Help:

Man ls

Info date

Command Line History

Practice Questions and Answers

Chapter 4: Vim Editor

Basic Navigation:

Editing in Vim:

Search and Replacement:

Copying and Pasting:

Practice Questions and Answers

Chapter 5: Linux Files and Directories

Practice Questions and Answers

Chapter 6: Managing Linux Users

Root Account:

Creating Users:

Modifying Users:

Changing Passwords:

Practice Questions and Answers

Chapter 7: Linux Groups

Creating Groups:

Modifying Groups:

Administering Groups:

ls Command:

Practice Questions and Answers

Chapter 8: Manage Software Applications

RPM Package Manager:

Advanced Packaging Tool (APT):

Practice Questions and Answers

Chapter 9: Managing Processes

Listing Running Processes:

Background Processes:

Backgrounding Foreground Processes:

Killing Processes:

Practice Questions and Answers

Chapter 10: Networking in Linux

Network Configuration:

Network Troubleshooting:

Network Services:

Chapter 11: Permissions

Changing File Ownership:

Permissions Basics:

Modifying File Permissions:

Practice Questions and Answers

Chapter 12: Hardware Management

Interrupt Request (IRQ):

I/O Ports:

Kernel Modules:

Loading Kernel Modules:

Removing Kernel Modules:

Getting CPU Info:

Getting System Information:

USB Devices:

Hard Disks Configuration:

Creating a New Partition:

Practice Questions and Answers

Chapter 13: Booting Linux

GRUB version 1:

Configuring Grub Legacy:

GRUB Version 2:

Linux Runlevels:

Practice Question and Answers

Conclusion

Introduction

In the realm of information technology, proficiency in operating systems is paramount. Among the plethora of operating systems available, Linux stands out for its robustness, versatility, and widespread usage across various platforms. Recognizing the significance of Linux expertise, the CompTIA Linux+ certification serves as a definitive benchmark for validating the skills of IT professionals in administering Linux systems.

This book is meticulously crafted to aid aspirants in their journey towards mastering the CompTIA Linux+ certification. Packed with a comprehensive array of practice questions and detailed answers, it serves as an indispensable resource for honing one's understanding of Linux essentials, system configuration, command-line interface proficiency, shell scripting, security administration, and much more.

Designed to emulate the format and rigor of the actual examination, each practice question is thoughtfully constructed to challenge and reinforce the reader's comprehension of critical concepts. Through a systematic approach, readers are afforded the opportunity to solidify their grasp of Linux fundamentals while gaining valuable insights into the nuances of real-world scenarios.

Whether you're a seasoned IT professional seeking to formalize your Linux expertise or an aspiring newcomer looking to embark on a career in system administration, this book equips you with the tools and knowledge necessary to excel in the CompTIA Linux+ certification examination. Embrace the challenge, delve into the intricacies of Linux administration, and embark on a transformative journey towards professional excellence.

In the ever-evolving landscape of information technology, proficiency in operating systems is a cornerstone skill for IT professionals. Among the myriad of operating systems available, Linux stands tall, revered for its robustness, flexibility, and omnipresence across diverse platforms. As organizations increasingly rely on Linux-based infrastructures to power their operations, the demand for skilled Linux administrators continues to surge. Recognizing the pivotal role of Linux expertise in the modern IT ecosystem, CompTIA, a leading provider of IT certifications, introduced the Linux+ certification to validate the skills and knowledge of professionals in administering Linux systems.

This comprehensive guide is meticulously curated to serve as an invaluable companion to aspiring Linux professionals on their journey towards achieving the esteemed CompTIA Linux+ certification. Drawing upon years of collective experience and expertise in Linux administration, this book offers a wealth of practice questions, detailed answers, and insightful explanations to equip readers with the requisite skills to excel in the certification examination and beyond.

To embark on any journey, it is essential to understand the destination. In this chapter, we delve into the intricacies of the CompTIA Linux+ certification, exploring its significance, objectives, and the skills it aims to validate. From foundational Linux concepts to advanced system administration tasks, we provide a roadmap to navigate the certification landscape effectively.

At the heart of Linux proficiency lies a solid understanding of its fundamental principles. In this chapter, we delve into the core concepts that underpin the Linux operating system, including file system hierarchy, user and group management, permissions, and package management. Through a series of practice questions and hands-on exercises, readers will reinforce their understanding of these essential concepts, laying a robust foundation for further exploration.

The command line interface (CLI) is a powerful tool that lies at the essence of Linux administration. In this chapter, we delve into the intricacies of the Linux command line, covering essential commands, command syntax, piping, redirection, and scripting basics. By immersing themselves in practical exercises and challenging practice questions, readers will sharpen their command line skills, enabling them to navigate and manipulate Linux systems with confidence and efficiency.

Effective system configuration and maintenance are critical components of Linux administration. In this chapter, we explore key tasks such as system boot processes, kernel management, network configuration, and system monitoring. Through a series of practice questions that mirror real-world scenarios, readers will gain practical insights into optimizing system performance, troubleshooting common issues, and ensuring the reliability and stability of Linux-based infrastructures.

User management is a cornerstone aspect of Linux administration, influencing security, access control, and resource allocation. In this chapter, we delve into the intricacies of user account management, group administration, file permissions, and privilege escalation. By tackling challenging practice questions and scenarios, readers will refine their user management skills, mastering the art of balancing security requirements with operational efficiency.

Security is paramount in any IT environment, and Linux systems are no exception. In this chapter, we explore a myriad of security measures, including firewall configuration, encryption, access control lists, and security best practices. Through hands-on exercises and real-world scenarios, readers will hone their security administration skills, fortifying Linux-based infrastructures against potential threats and vulnerabilities.

Automation lies at the heart of efficient system administration, enabling administrators to streamline repetitive tasks and enhance productivity. In this chapter, we delve into the world of shell scripting, exploring shell basics, scripting constructs, variables, flow control, and debugging techniques. By immersing themselves in practical scripting exercises and complex scenarios, readers will acquire the skills to automate tasks effectively, empowering them to become proficient Linux administrators.

As the culmination of their journey approaches, it is essential for readers to prepare diligently for the CompTIA Linux+ certification examination. In this chapter, we offer practical tips, study strategies, and exam preparation techniques to help readers maximize their chances of success. From creating a study plan to leveraging practice exams and mock tests, we provide guidance to ensure readers enter the examination room with confidence and readiness.

CompTIA Linux+ certification is not merely about passing an exam; it is a transformative odyssey that equips aspiring Linux professionals with the skills, knowledge, and confidence to excel in their careers. Through diligent study, hands-on practice, and unwavering determination, readers will emerge from this journey as adept Linux administrators, poised to tackle the challenges of the ever-evolving IT landscape with aplomb. Embark on this journey with zeal and dedication, and let the pursuit of excellence propel you towards professional success and fulfillment..

Chapter 1: Introduction to Linux

Linux, an open-source operating system kernel initially developed by Linus Torvalds in 1991, has since evolved into a global phenomenon, powering a vast array of devices, servers, and systems worldwide. Understanding the fundamentals of Linux is essential for anyone seeking to navigate the intricate world of modern computing.

What is Linux?

Linux is an operating system kernel, the core component responsible for managing hardware resources, facilitating communication between software applications and the underlying hardware, and providing essential services to users. Unlike proprietary operating systems such as Windows or macOS, Linux is open-source, meaning its source code is freely available for inspection, modification, and redistribution by anyone under the terms of its licensing agreements.

What is an Operating System?

An operating system (OS) is a software layer that acts as an intermediary between computer hardware and user applications, providing a platform for executing programs, managing system resources, and facilitating user interaction. Essential functions performed by an operating system include process management, memory allocation, file system management, device input/output (I/O) handling, and security enforcement.

How was Linux Developed?

The development of Linux traces its roots back to the early 1990s when Linus Torvalds, a Finnish computer science student, embarked on a personal project to create a Unix-like operating system kernel. Inspired by the Unix operating system and dissatisfied with the limitations of proprietary operating systems available at the time, Torvalds set out to develop a kernel that would be freely available, collaboratively developed, and customizable to suit diverse computing needs.

Linux and GNU System

One of the defining aspects of Linux is its association with the GNU project, an ambitious initiative launched by Richard Stallman and the Free Software Foundation (FSF) in the mid-1980s to develop a complete Unix-like operating system composed entirely of free software. While the GNU project made significant strides in developing essential software components such as compilers, text editors, and utilities, it lacked a kernel to bring these components together into a functional operating system.

Enter Linux: Linus Torvalds' kernel project provided the missing piece of the puzzle for the GNU system. By combining the Linux kernel with GNU's user-space utilities and tools, developers were able to create a fully functional, Unix-compatible operating system known as GNU/Linux or simply Linux. This collaborative effort between the Linux kernel and GNU software laid the foundation for the open-source ecosystem that thrives today, empowering users with freedom, flexibility, and control over their computing environments.

Linux is a powerful, open-source operating system kernel that has revolutionized the world of computing. Developed by Linus Torvalds and supported by a vibrant community of developers worldwide, Linux offers users a robust, customizable platform for a wide range of computing tasks. Its integration with the GNU project's user-space utilities underscores the collaborative spirit of open-source software development, making Linux a cornerstone of the modern computing landscape.

Linux Distributions:

Linux distributions, commonly referred to as "distros," are complete operating system packages that include the Linux kernel along with a collection of software applications, utilities, libraries, and graphical interfaces tailored to specific user needs and preferences. There are hundreds of Linux distributions available, each with its unique characteristics, target audiences, and usage scenarios. Some popular Linux distributions include Ubuntu, Debian, Fedora, CentOS, Arch Linux, and openSUSE, among others.

Linux Implementations:

Linux implementations encompass a broad spectrum of computing environments and use cases, ranging from desktop computers and servers to embedded systems and mobile devices. Each implementation is customized to meet the requirements of its intended platform, leveraging the flexibility and versatility of the Linux kernel to deliver optimal performance, reliability, and functionality.

Linux Desktop:

The Linux desktop environment provides users with a graphical user interface (GUI) for interacting with their computer systems, offering a wide range of productivity tools, multimedia applications, and customization options. Popular Linux desktop environments include GNOME, KDE Plasma, Xfce, LXDE, and Cinnamon, each offering a unique user experience and feature set. Linux desktop distributions such as Ubuntu, Fedora, and Linux Mint cater to desktop users' needs, providing a user-friendly interface coupled with robust performance and software availability.

Linux Server:

Linux servers form the backbone of the internet, powering a vast array of websites, web applications, cloud services, and enterprise infrastructure. Linux's reliability, scalability, and security make it the preferred choice for server deployments across industries. Server-oriented Linux distributions such as CentOS, Ubuntu Server, and Red Hat Enterprise Linux offer optimized configurations and package selections tailored to server workloads, providing administrators with the tools and resources to build robust and efficient server infrastructures.

Mobile Linux:

Mobile Linux refers to the use of Linux-based operating systems on mobile devices such as smartphones, tablets, and wearable devices. Android, developed by Google and based on the Linux kernel, is the most widely used mobile Linux platform, commanding a significant share of the global smartphone market. Android's open-source nature, extensive app ecosystem, and customization options have made it a popular choice among device manufacturers and consumers alike.

Embedded Linux:

Embedded Linux is utilized in embedded systems, specialized computing devices designed for specific tasks or applications. Embedded Linux distributions are tailored to the constraints of embedded hardware, offering lightweight, customizable solutions for embedded development projects. Embedded Linux finds applications in a wide range of industries, including consumer electronics, automotive, industrial automation, and IoT (Internet of Things) devices.

Linux and Virtualization:

Linux plays a crucial role in the field of virtualization, enabling the creation and management of virtualized environments on physical hardware. Virtualization technologies such as KVM (Kernel-based Virtual Machine), Xen, and VMware leverage the Linux kernel's support for virtualization to provide efficient and scalable virtualization solutions for enterprise and cloud computing environments. Linux-based virtualization platforms offer features such as resource isolation, live migration, and virtual networking, empowering organizations to optimize resource utilization, improve infrastructure flexibility, and streamline management tasks.

Linux distributions and implementations encompass a diverse array of computing environments, each tailored to meet specific user needs and usage scenarios. Whether it's powering desktop computers, servers, mobile devices, embedded systems, or virtualized environments, Linux's versatility, reliability, and flexibility make it a ubiquitous and indispensable component of the modern computing landscape.

Practice Questions and Answers

What is Linux?

a) A proprietary operating system

b) An open-source operating system kernel

c) A graphical user interface

d) A programming language

Answer: b) An open-source operating system kernel

Explanation: Linux is not a proprietary operating system; it is open-source, meaning its source code is freely available for inspection, modification, and redistribution. It is not a graphical user interface or a programming language; instead, it is an operating system kernel that manages hardware resources and facilitates communication between software applications and the underlying hardware.

What is the primary function of an operating system?

a) Managing hardware resources

b) Providing a graphical user interface

c) Running applications

d) Playing multimedia files

Answer: a) Managing hardware resources

Explanation: While an operating system may provide a graphical user interface and run applications, its primary function is to manage hardware resources such as CPU, memory, disk storage, and peripherals. This includes tasks such as process management, memory allocation, device management, and file system handling.

Who initially developed the Linux kernel?

a) Bill Gates

b) Steve Jobs

c) Linus Torvalds

d) Richard Stallman

Answer: c) Linus Torvalds

Explanation: Linus Torvalds, a Finnish computer science student, developed the Linux kernel in 1991 as a personal project. His goal was to create a Unix-like operating system kernel that would be freely available and collaboratively developed by the open-source community.

What is the GNU project?

a) A hardware manufacturer

b) A software development project

c) A government agency

d) A financial institution

Answer: b) A software development project

Explanation: The GNU project, launched by Richard Stallman and the Free Software Foundation (FSF), aims to develop a complete Unix-like operating system composed entirely of free software. While Linux provides the kernel for GNU/Linux distributions, the GNU project contributes essential user-space utilities, libraries, and tools to create a fully functional operating system.

What is the combination of the Linux kernel and GNU software called?

a) Windows

b) macOS

c) GNU/Linux or Linux

d) Unix

Answer: c) GNU/Linux or Linux

Explanation: The combination of the Linux kernel and GNU software forms a complete operating system known as GNU/Linux or simply Linux. This collaboration between the Linux kernel and GNU project software provides users with a robust, customizable platform for various computing tasks.

Which of the following is not a popular Linux distribution?

a) Ubuntu

b) Windows

c) Fedora

d) Debian

Answer: b) Windows

Explanation: Windows is a proprietary operating system developed by Microsoft and is not a Linux distribution. Ubuntu, Fedora, and Debian are popular Linux distributions, each offering a unique set of features, package management systems, and user interfaces.

What is the purpose of a Linux distribution?

a) To provide a graphical user interface

b) To develop software applications

c) To package the Linux kernel with software and utilities

d) To manufacture computer hardware

Answer: c) To package the Linux kernel with software and utilities

Explanation: A Linux distribution packages the Linux kernel with additional software, utilities, libraries, and a package management system to provide a complete operating system for users. Different distributions cater to various needs, preferences, and usage scenarios, offering distinct features, desktop environments, and package selections.

Which of the following is not a Linux desktop environment?

a) GNOME

b) KDE Plasma

c) Xfce

d) Apache

Answer: d) Apache

Explanation: Apache is not a Linux desktop environment; it is a popular open-source web server software used for hosting websites and web applications. GNOME, KDE Plasma, and Xfce are examples of Linux desktop environments, each providing a graphical user interface and a set of integrated applications for desktop computing.

What is the primary function of a Linux server?

a) Running desktop applications

b) Hosting websites and web applications

c) Playing multimedia files

d) Gaming

Answer: b) Hosting websites and web applications

Explanation: A Linux server is designed to host websites, web applications, and other network services, providing reliable, scalable, and secure infrastructure for businesses, organizations, and individuals. While Linux servers can perform various tasks, their primary function is to serve content and services over the network.

Which mobile operating system is based on the Linux kernel?

a) iOS

b) Android

c) Windows Phone

d) BlackBerry OS

Answer: b) Android

Explanation: Android is a mobile operating system developed by Google, based on the Linux kernel. It is the most widely used mobile Linux platform, powering a significant portion of smartphones, tablets, and other mobile devices worldwide.

What type of devices typically use Embedded Linux?

a) Desktop computers

b) Servers

c) Smartphones

d) IoT devices

Answer: d) IoT devices

Explanation: Embedded Linux is commonly used in embedded systems, specialized computing devices designed for specific tasks or applications. Examples of embedded Linux applications include smart appliances, industrial automation systems, IoT devices, and embedded controllers.

What role does Linux play in virtualization?

a) Providing virtual reality experiences

b) Hosting virtual private networks (VPNs)

c) Enabling the creation and management of virtualized environments

d) Running emulators for legacy operating systems

Answer: c) Enabling the creation and management of virtualized environments

Explanation: Linux provides the foundation for virtualization technologies such as KVM (Kernel-based Virtual Machine), Xen, and VMware, allowing users to create, manage, and run virtualized environments on physical hardware. Virtualization enables organizations to consolidate resources, improve hardware utilization, and streamline management tasks by running multiple virtual machines on a single physical server.

What distinguishes Linux from proprietary operating systems?

a) Linux is developed by Microsoft

b) Linux is free and open-source

c) Linux has a graphical user interface

d) Linux is only used on servers

Answer: b) Linux is free and open-source

Explanation: Unlike proprietary operating systems, Linux is free and open-source, meaning its source code is freely available for inspection, modification, and redistribution. This allows users to customize Linux to suit their needs, contribute improvements to the codebase, and redistribute modified versions of the operating system.

What is the primary advantage of using Linux for server deployments?

a) Lower hardware requirements

b) Greater compatibility with proprietary software

c) Enhanced security features

d) Exclusive support for Microsoft products

Answer: c) Enhanced security features

Explanation: Linux servers are known for their robust security features, including access controls, filesystem permissions, and security-enhanced kernels. Linux distributions receive regular security updates and patches, and the open-source nature of Linux allows security vulnerabilities to be identified and addressed promptly by the community.

What distinguishes Linux from other operating systems in terms of customization?

a) Linux allows users to modify the source code

b) Linux has a fixed user interface

c) Linux restricts access to system settings

d) Linux only supports a limited number of software applications

Answer: a) Linux allows users to modify the source code

Explanation: Linux's open-source nature allows users to access and modify the source code of the operating system and its associated software. This level of customization enables users to tailor Linux to their specific requirements, preferences, and usage scenarios, making it highly flexible and adaptable compared to proprietary operating systems.

Which of the following components is essential for creating a Linux distribution?

a) A graphical user interface

b) A package management system

c) A web browser

d) A word processor

Answer: b) A package management system

Explanation: A package management system is essential for creating a Linux distribution as it facilitates the installation, upgrade, and removal of software packages on the system. Package management systems such as apt (used in Debian-based distributions), yum (used in Red Hat-based distributions), and pacman (used in Arch Linux) automate the process of software management, ensuring system integrity and dependency resolution.

What distinguishes Linux from other operating systems in terms of licensing?

a) Linux is proprietary software

b) Linux is governed by the GPL (GNU General Public License)

c) Linux requires a paid license for commercial use

d) Linux is developed by a single corporation

Answer: b) Linux is governed by the GPL (GNU General Public License)

Explanation: Linux is governed by the GNU General Public License (GPL), a free software license that grants users the freedom to run, study, modify, and redistribute the software. The GPL ensures that Linux remains open-source and freely accessible to all users, fostering collaboration, innovation, and community-driven development.

What role does the Linux kernel play in the operating system?

a) Managing hardware resources

b) Providing a graphical user interface

c) Running applications

d) Playing multimedia files

Answer: a) Managing hardware resources

Explanation: The Linux kernel is the core component of the Linux operating system responsible for managing hardware resources such as CPU, memory, disk storage, and peripherals. It provides essential services to user-space applications, including process management, memory allocation, device drivers, and system calls.

Which of the following is not a common Linux desktop environment?

a) GNOME

b) KDE Plasma

c) Xfce

d) Apache

Answer: d) Apache

Explanation: Apache is not a Linux desktop environment; it is a popular open-source web server software used for hosting websites and web applications. GNOME, KDE Plasma, and Xfce are examples of Linux desktop environments, each providing a graphical user interface and a set of integrated applications for desktop computing.

What is the primary benefit of using Linux for embedded systems?

a) Greater compatibility with proprietary software

b) Lower hardware requirements

c) Enhanced security features

d) Exclusive support for Microsoft products

Answer: c) Enhanced security features

Explanation: Linux's robust security features make it well-suited for use in embedded systems, where reliability, stability, and security are paramount. Linux-based embedded systems benefit from features such as access controls, filesystem permissions, and security-enhanced kernels, protecting them from potential security threats and vulnerabilities.

What distinguishes Linux from proprietary operating systems in terms of licensing?

a) Linux requires a paid license for commercial use

b) Linux is governed by the GPL (GNU General Public License)

c) Linux is developed by a single corporation

d) Linux is proprietary software

Answer: b) Linux is governed by the GPL (GNU General Public License)

Explanation: Linux is governed by the GNU General Public License (GPL), a free software license that grants users the freedom to run, study, modify, and redistribute the software. Unlike proprietary operating systems, Linux remains open-source and freely accessible to all users, fostering collaboration, innovation, and community-driven development.

What distinguishes Linux from other operating systems in terms of customization?

a) Linux allows users to modify the source code

b) Linux has a fixed user interface

c) Linux restricts access to system settings

d) Linux only supports a limited number of software applications

Answer: a) Linux allows users to modify the source code

Explanation: Linux's open-source nature allows users to access and modify the source code of the operating system and its associated software. This level of customization enables users to tailor Linux to their specific requirements, preferences, and usage scenarios, making it highly flexible and adaptable compared to proprietary operating systems.

What is the primary function of an operating system?

a) Running applications

b) Providing a graphical user interface

c) Managing hardware resources

d) Playing multimedia files

Answer: c) Managing hardware resources

Explanation: While an operating system may provide a graphical user interface and run applications, its primary function is to manage hardware resources such as CPU, memory, disk storage, and peripherals. This includes tasks such as process management, memory allocation, device management, and file system handling.

What is the purpose of a Linux distribution?

a) To provide a graphical user interface

b) To develop software applications

c) To package the Linux kernel with software and utilities

d) To manufacture computer hardware

Answer: c) To package the Linux kernel with software and utilities

Explanation: A Linux distribution packages the Linux kernel with additional software, utilities, libraries, and a package management system to provide a complete operating system for users. Different distributions cater to various needs, preferences, and usage scenarios, offering distinct features, desktop environments, and package selections.

What is the combination of the Linux kernel and GNU software called?

a) Windows

b) macOS

c) GNU/Linux or Linux

d) Unix

Answer: c) GNU/Linux or Linux

Explanation: The combination of the Linux kernel and GNU software forms a complete operating system known as GNU/Linux or simply Linux. This collaboration between the Linux kernel and GNU project software provides users with a robust, customizable platform for various computing tasks.

What distinguishes Linux from proprietary operating systems in terms of licensing?

a) Linux is proprietary software

b) Linux is governed by the GPL (GNU General Public License)

c) Linux requires a paid license for commercial use

d) Linux is developed by a single corporation

Answer: b) Linux is governed by the GPL (GNU General Public License)

Explanation: Linux is governed by the GNU General Public License (GPL), a free software license that grants users the freedom to run, study, modify, and redistribute the software. The GPL ensures that Linux remains open-source and freely accessible to all users, fostering collaboration, innovation, and community-driven development.

What is the primary benefit of using Linux for server deployments?

a) Lower hardware requirements

b) Greater compatibility with proprietary software

c) Enhanced security features

d) Exclusive support for Microsoft products

Answer: c) Enhanced security features

Explanation: Linux servers are known for their robust security features, including access controls, filesystem permissions, and security-enhanced kernels. Linux distributions receive regular security updates and patches, and the open-source nature of Linux allows security vulnerabilities to be identified and addressed promptly by the community.

What distinguishes Linux from other operating systems in terms of customization?

a) Linux allows users to modify the source code

b) Linux has a fixed user interface

c) Linux restricts access to system settings

d) Linux only supports a limited number of software applications

Answer: a) Linux allows users to modify the source code

Explanation: Linux's open-source nature allows users to access and modify the source code of the operating system and its associated software. This level of customization enables users to tailor Linux to their specific requirements, preferences, and usage scenarios, making it highly flexible and adaptable compared to proprietary operating systems.

What is the primary function of an operating system?

a) Running applications

b) Providing a graphical user interface

c) Managing hardware resources

d) Playing multimedia files

Answer: c) Managing hardware resources

Explanation: While an operating system may provide a graphical user interface and run applications, its primary function is to manage hardware resources such as CPU, memory, disk storage, and peripherals. This includes tasks such as process management, memory allocation, device management, and file system handling.

What is the purpose of a Linux distribution?

a) To provide a graphical user interface

b) To develop software applications

c) To package the Linux kernel with software and utilities

d) To manufacture computer hardware

Answer: c) To package the Linux kernel with software and utilities

Explanation: A Linux distribution packages the Linux kernel with additional software, utilities, libraries, and a package management system to provide a complete operating system for users. Different distributions cater to various needs, preferences, and usage scenarios, offering distinct features, desktop environments, and package selections.

Chapter 2: Installing Linux

Installing Linux is a pivotal step towards harnessing the power and flexibility of this versatile operating system. Whether you're setting up a desktop workstation, configuring a server, or experimenting with different distributions, understanding the installation process is essential. This chapter provides a comprehensive guide to installing Linux, covering everything from system requirements to post-installation configuration.

System Requirements:

Before installing Linux, it's crucial to ensure that your hardware meets the necessary requirements. These requirements vary depending on the distribution and intended use case. Generally, you'll need a compatible processor (such as x86, ARM, or PowerPC), sufficient RAM (typically 1GB or more for desktop installations), available disk space for the operating system and applications, and compatible peripherals (keyboard, mouse, monitor, network interface, etc.). Some distributions may have specific hardware compatibility lists or recommendations, so it's advisable to consult the documentation or website of your chosen distribution for detailed requirements.

Choosing a Distribution:

Linux offers a diverse array of distributions, each tailored to specific user needs, preferences, and usage scenarios. Before proceeding with the installation, take the time to research and select a distribution that aligns with your requirements. Consider factors such as desktop environment (GNOME, KDE, Xfce, etc.), package management system (apt, yum, pacman, etc.), community support, stability, and software availability. Popular desktop-oriented distributions include Ubuntu, Fedora, Linux Mint, and elementary OS, while server-focused distributions include CentOS, Debian, Ubuntu Server, and Red Hat Enterprise Linux (RHEL).

Installation Media:

Once you've chosen a distribution, you'll need to obtain installation media. Most Linux distributions provide downloadable ISO images that can be burned to a DVD or written to a USB flash drive using specialized software like Rufus, Etcher, or dd. Alternatively, some distributions offer live images that allow you to boot into a live environment directly from the installation media, providing a preview of the distribution before installation.

Installation Process:

The installation process may vary slightly depending on the chosen distribution, but it typically involves the following steps:

a) Booting from the Installation Media: Insert the installation DVD or USB flash drive into your computer and boot from it. You may need to adjust the boot order in the BIOS or UEFI settings to prioritize the installation media.

b) Selecting Installation Options: Once the installation media boots, you'll be presented with various installation options, including language selection, keyboard layout, timezone configuration, and disk partitioning. Follow the on-screen prompts to customize these settings according to your preferences.

c) Disk Partitioning: Partitioning your disk is a critical step in the installation process. You can choose to use the entire disk for Linux, dual-boot with another operating system, or manually partition the disk to suit your needs. Most distributions offer guided partitioning options for beginners and advanced partitioning tools for experienced users.

d) Installing the System: After configuring the installation options and disk partitions, proceed with the installation process. This may involve copying files from the installation media to the hard drive, configuring system settings, and installing bootloader software (such as GRUB or systemd-boot) to enable booting into Linux.

e) Post-Installation Configuration: Once the installation is complete, you may need to perform additional configuration steps, such as setting up user accounts, configuring network settings, installing additional software packages, and updating the system software. Many distributions provide post-installation wizards or tools to streamline these tasks and ensure a smooth transition to the installed system.

Troubleshooting:

Despite the straightforward nature of the installation process, you may encounter issues or errors along the way. Common troubleshooting steps include verifying hardware compatibility, checking installation media integrity, adjusting BIOS/UEFI settings, troubleshooting disk partitioning issues, and consulting online forums or documentation for solutions to specific problems. Most distributions also offer live support channels, IRC chat rooms, or community forums where users can seek assistance from experienced users and developers.

By following these steps and guidelines, you can successfully install Linux on your computer or server, paving the way for a rewarding and productive computing experience. Whether you're a seasoned Linux user or a newcomer to the world of open-source software, the installation process serves as a gateway to unlocking the full potential of Linux and embracing the freedom, flexibility, and innovation that it offers.

Practice Questions and Answers

What are the minimum system requirements for installing most Linux distributions?

a) 512MB RAM and 5GB disk space

b) 1GB RAM and 10GB disk space

c) 2GB RAM and 20GB disk space

d) 4GB RAM and 50GB disk space

Answer: b) 1GB RAM and 10GB disk space

Explanation: Most Linux distributions require at least 1GB of RAM and 10GB of disk space for installation. These requirements may vary slightly depending on the distribution and intended use case.

Which of the following is NOT a popular Linux distribution?

a) Ubuntu

b) Fedora

c) CentOS

d) Windows

Answer: d) Windows

Explanation: Windows is a proprietary operating system developed by Microsoft and is not a Linux distribution.

What is the purpose of the Linux distribution?

a) To provide a graphical user interface

b) To develop software applications

c) To package the Linux kernel with software and utilities

d) To manufacture computer hardware

Answer: c) To package the Linux kernel with software and utilities

Explanation: A Linux distribution packages the Linux kernel with additional software, utilities, libraries, and a package management system to provide a complete operating system for users.

What tool can be used to burn a Linux ISO image to a USB flash drive?

a) WinRAR

b) Rufus

c) Disk Utility

d) WinZip

Answer: b) Rufus

Explanation: Rufus is a popular tool for creating bootable USB flash drives from ISO images, including Linux distributions.

What is the first step in the Linux installation process?

a) Partitioning the disk

b) Configuring system settings

c) Booting from the installation media

d) Installing additional software packages

Answer: c) Booting from the installation media

Explanation: The first step in the Linux installation process is to boot from the installation media, such as a DVD or USB flash drive.

Which partitioning scheme allows for dual-booting Linux with another operating system?

a) GUID Partition Table (GPT)

b) Master Boot Record (MBR)

c) Logical Volume Manager (LVM)

d) ZFS

Answer: b) Master Boot Record (MBR)

Explanation: Master Boot Record (MBR) partitioning scheme allows for dual-booting Linux with another operating system by creating separate partitions for each OS.

Which bootloader is commonly used with Linux installations?

a) Windows Boot Manager

b) GRUB (Grand Unified Bootloader)

c) LILO (Linux Loader)

d) systemd-boot

Answer: b) GRUB (Grand Unified Bootloader)

Explanation: GRUB (Grand Unified Bootloader) is commonly used as the bootloader for Linux installations, allowing users to choose which operating system to boot at startup.

What is the purpose of the swap partition in Linux?

a) To store temporary files

b) To provide additional disk space

c) To act as virtual memory

d) To store system configuration files

Answer: c) To act as virtual memory

Explanation: The swap partition in Linux serves as virtual memory, allowing the system to use disk space as additional RAM when physical memory (RAM) is insufficient.

What command is used to update the package repository in Debian-based Linux distributions?

a) apt-get update

b) yum update

c) pacman -Syu

d) dnf update

Answer: a) apt-get update

Explanation: The "apt-get update" command is used to update the package repository in Debian-based Linux distributions, such as Ubuntu and Debian.

Which desktop environment is the default in Ubuntu Linux?

a) GNOME

b) KDE Plasma

c) Xfce

d) LXQt

Answer: a) GNOME

Explanation: GNOME is the default desktop environment in Ubuntu Linux, providing a user-friendly interface and a set of integrated applications.

What is the purpose of the Linux kernel?

a) To provide a graphical user interface

b) To manage hardware resources

c) To run applications

d) To provide networking services

Answer: b) To manage hardware resources

Explanation: The Linux kernel is responsible for managing hardware resources, including CPU, memory, disk storage, and peripherals.

Which of the following is NOT a common file system used in Linux?

a) NTFS

b) ext4

c) XFS

d) Btrfs

Answer: a) NTFS

Explanation: NTFS is a file system commonly used in Windows operating systems and is not commonly used in Linux.

What is the purpose of the GRUB bootloader?

a) To provide a graphical user interface

b) To manage hardware resources

c) To load the Linux kernel and initiate the boot process

d) To configure system settings

Answer: c) To load the Linux kernel and initiate the boot process

Explanation: GRUB (Grand Unified Bootloader) is responsible for loading the Linux kernel and initiating the boot process, allowing users to choose which operating system to boot at startup.

Which of the following is NOT a benefit of using Linux?

a) Open-source nature

b) Enhanced security features

c) Limited software availability

d) Customization options

Answer: c) Limited software availability

Explanation: One of the benefits of using Linux is its wide range of available software, including thousands of free and open-source applications.

What is the primary function of the package management system in Linux?

a) To provide a graphical user interface

b) To manage hardware resources

c) To install, update, and remove software packages

d) To configure system settings

Answer: c) To install, update, and remove software packages

Explanation: The package management system in Linux is responsible for installing, updating, and removing software packages, as well as resolving dependencies and managing repositories.

Which Linux command is used to list the contents of a directory?

a) ls

b) cd

c) cp

d) mv

Answer: a) ls

Explanation: The "ls" command is used to list the contents of a directory in Linux.

What is the purpose of the sudo command in Linux?

a) To switch between user accounts

b) To view system logs

c) To run commands with elevated privileges

d) To compress files and directories

Answer: c) To run commands with elevated privileges

Explanation: The sudo command in Linux allows users to run commands with elevated privileges, typically requiring authentication with a password.

Which command is used to create a new directory in Linux?

a) mkdir

b) touch

c) rm

d) rmdir

Answer: a) mkdir

Explanation: The "mkdir" command is used to create a new directory in Linux.

What is the purpose of the chmod command in Linux?

a) To change file ownership

b) To change file permissions

c) To compress files

d) To rename files

Answer: b) To change file permissions

Explanation: The chmod command in Linux is used to change the permissions (read, write, execute) of files and directories.

What does the acronym GUI stand for in Linux?

a) Graphical User Interface

b) Global User Interaction

c) Graphical Utility Interface

d) General User Integration

Answer: a) Graphical User Interface

Explanation: GUI stands for Graphical User Interface, which provides a visual way for users to interact with the operating system and applications.

Which command is used to shut down a Linux system?

a) shutdown

b) poweroff

c) halt

d) All of the above

Answer: d) All of the above

Explanation: All of the mentioned commands can be used to shut down a Linux system.

Which Linux command is used to display the contents of a text file?

a) cat

b) grep

c) less

d) head

Answer: a) cat

Explanation: The "cat" command is used to display the contents of a text file in Linux.

What does the acronym SSH stand for in Linux?

a) Secure Shell

b) Superuser Shell

c) System Services Hub

d) Secure Socket Host

Answer: a) Secure Shell

Explanation: SSH stands for Secure Shell, a cryptographic network protocol used for secure communication between two computers.

Which Linux command is used to copy files and directories?

a) cp

b) mv

c) rm

d) touch

Answer: a) cp

Explanation: The "cp" command is used to copy files and directories in Linux.

What is the purpose of the df command in Linux?

a) To display disk usage statistics

b) To display system information

c) To display CPU usage

d) To display network connections

Answer: a) To display disk usage statistics

Explanation: The df command in Linux is used to display disk usage statistics, including disk space usage and available space on mounted file systems.

Which Linux command is used to change the current directory?

a) cd

b) pwd

c) ls

d) mv

Answer: a) cd

Explanation: The "cd" command is used to change the current directory in Linux.

What is the purpose of the uptime command in Linux?

a) To display the current date and time

b) To display the system's uptime

c) To display system resource usage

d) To display the system's boot time

Answer: b) To display the system's uptime

Explanation: The uptime command in Linux is used to display the system's uptime, indicating how long the system has been running since the last reboot.

Which Linux command is used to create an empty file?

a) touch

b) mkdir

c) cp

d) rm

Answer: a) touch

Explanation: The "touch" command is used to create an empty file in Linux.

What is the purpose of the grep command in Linux?

a) To search for text patterns in files

b) To display system logs

c) To compress files and directories

d) To change file permissions

Answer: a) To search for text patterns in files

Explanation: The grep command in Linux is used to search for text patterns in files and display matching lines.

Which Linux command is used to remove files and directories?

a) rm

b) rmdir

c) rm -rf

d) All of the above

Answer: d) All of the above

Explanation: All of the mentioned commands can be used to remove files and directories in Linux.

Chapter 3: The Linux Shell

The Linux shell, often referred to as the command line interface (CLI), is a powerful tool for interacting with the operating system and executing commands. In this chapter, we explore the fundamentals of the Linux shell, including basic terminal editing, auto-completion, and accessing help resources.

Basic Terminal Editing:

The Linux shell provides various keyboard shortcuts and commands for efficient terminal editing. Users can navigate through command history, edit commands, and perform text manipulation tasks using key combinations such as Ctrl + A (move to the beginning of the line), Ctrl + E (move to the end of the line), Ctrl + U (delete from the cursor to the beginning of the line), and Ctrl + K (delete from the cursor to the end of the line). Understanding these basic editing commands enhances productivity and workflow efficiency when working in the terminal.

Auto-Completion:

Auto-completion is a feature of the Linux shell that helps users quickly complete commands, file paths, and other arguments by pressing the Tab key. When typing a command or file path, pressing Tab will automatically complete the input based on available options, reducing typing effort and minimizing errors. Additionally, users can press Tab twice to display a list of possible completions if multiple options exist. Leveraging auto-completion streamlines command entry and enhances command line usability, particularly for repetitive tasks and navigating file systems.

Getting Help:

The Linux shell provides several methods for accessing help resources and documentation to assist users in understanding commands, options, and syntax. The most common way to obtain help is by using the man (manual) command followed by the name of the command or topic of interest (e.g., man ls). This displays the manual page for the specified command, providing detailed information on usage, options, and examples. Alternatively, users can use the --help option with most commands to display a brief summary of usage and available options directly in the terminal. Additionally, online resources, community forums, and official documentation websites offer valuable support and guidance for Linux users seeking assistance with specific commands or troubleshooting issues.

Understanding basic terminal editing, leveraging auto-completion, and accessing help resources empower Linux users to navigate the shell efficiently, execute commands effectively, and troubleshoot issues confidently. By mastering these essential skills, users can unlock the full potential of the Linux command line interface and maximize productivity in various computing environments.

Man ls

The ls command in Linux is used to list directory contents. It displays information about the files and directories within the specified directory. Below is a brief overview of the ls command:

Usage:

```
ls [OPTION]... [FILE]...
```

Options:

-a, --all: Show hidden files (files starting with a dot).

-l: Use a long listing format, showing detailed information about each file.

-h, --human-readable: Print sizes in human-readable format (e.g., 1K, 234M, 2G).

-r, --reverse: Reverse the order of the sort to get reverse lexicographical order.

-t: Sort files by modification time, newest first.

For more options and detailed information, refer to the manual page of ls by typing man ls in the terminal.

Info date

The date command in Linux is used to display or set the system date and time. It provides a way to display the current date and time or to set the system clock. Below is a brief overview of the date command:

Usage:

```
date [OPTION]... [+FORMAT]
```

Options:

-u, --utc, --universal: Display or set Coordinated Universal Time (UTC) instead of the local time.

+FORMAT: Specify a format to display the date and time. For example, %Y-%m-%d will display the date in the format YYYY-MM-DD.

For more options and detailed information, refer to the manual page of date by typing info date in the terminal.

Command Line History

The command line history in Linux stores a record of previously executed commands, allowing users to recall and re-execute commands conveniently. Here's how you can interact with the command line history:

Viewing Command History:

To view the command history, simply press the Up and Down arrow keys on your keyboard. This will cycle through previously executed commands.

Alternatively, you can use the history command to display a list of previously executed commands along with their line numbers.

Executing Previous Commands:

To execute a previously executed command again, you can press the Up arrow key to navigate to the desired command and then press Enter.

You can also use !n, where n is the line number of the command in the history, to execute a specific command from history.

Searching Command History:

Use Ctrl + R to search backward through the command history for a specific command. As you type, it will display the most recent matching command. Pressing Ctrl + R again will display the next matching command.

You can also use the history | grep keyword command to search for commands containing a specific keyword in the history.

Understanding how to navigate and utilize the command line history effectively can greatly improve your productivity and efficiency when working in the Linux shell.

Practice Questions and Answers

What command is used to list directory contents in Linux?

a) ls

b) cd

c) mv

d) cp

Answer: a) ls

Explanation: The ls command is used to list directory contents in Linux.

Which option is used with the ls command to display hidden files?

a) -a

b) -l

c) -h

d) -r

Answer: a) -a

Explanation: The -a option with the ls command is used to display hidden files (files starting with a dot).

What command is used to display the current date and time in Linux?

a) date

b) time

c) clock

d) datetime

Answer: a) date

Explanation: The date command is used to display the current date and time in Linux.

Which option with the date command is used to display the date and time in UTC (Coordinated Universal Time)?

a) -u

b) -utc

c) -universal

d) All of the above

Answer: d) All of the above

Explanation: Options -u, -utc, and -universal with the date command are used to display the date and time in UTC (Coordinated Universal Time).

How can you display the command line history in Linux?

a) history

b) hist

c) cmdhistory

d) hstry

Answer: a) history

Explanation: The history command is used to display the command line history in Linux.

Which key combination is used to search backward through the command history in Linux?

a) Ctrl + R

b) Ctrl + S

c) Ctrl + F

d) Ctrl + B

Answer: a) Ctrl + R

Explanation: Ctrl + R is used to search backward through the command history in Linux.

What command is used to move the cursor to the beginning of the line in the terminal?

a) Ctrl + A

b) Ctrl + E

c) Ctrl + U

d) Ctrl + K

Answer: a) Ctrl + A

Explanation: Ctrl + A moves the cursor to the beginning of the line in the terminal.

Which command is used to delete text from the cursor position to the beginning of the line in the terminal?

a) Ctrl + A

b) Ctrl + E

c) Ctrl + U

d) Ctrl + K

Answer: c) Ctrl + U

Explanation: Ctrl + U is used to delete text from the cursor position to the beginning of the line in the terminal.

Which option with the ls command is used to display file sizes in human-readable format?

a) -h

b) -s

c) -l

d) -r

Answer: a) -h

Explanation: The -h option with the ls command is used to display file sizes in human-readable format.

What is auto-completion in the Linux shell?

a) Automatically executing commands

b) Automatically completing file paths and command arguments

c) Automatically shutting down the system

d) Automatically updating system packages

Answer: b) Automatically completing file paths and command arguments

Explanation: Auto-completion in the Linux shell refers to automatically completing file paths and command arguments by pressing the Tab key.

Which command is used to set the system date and time in Linux?

a) setdate

b) timedatectl

c) date

d) settime

Answer: c) date

Explanation: The date command is used to set the system date and time in Linux.

What does the man command do in Linux?

a) Displays the system date and time

b) Displays manual pages for commands

c) Displays the command line history

d) Displays information about system hardware

Answer: b) Displays manual pages for commands

Explanation: The man command in Linux is used to display manual pages for commands, providing detailed information about their usage and options.

Which key combination is used to move the cursor to the end of the line in the terminal?

a) Ctrl + A

b) Ctrl + E

c) Ctrl + U

d) Ctrl + K

Answer: b) Ctrl + E

Explanation: Ctrl + E is used to move the cursor to the end of the line in the terminal.

What is the purpose of the grep command in Linux?

a) To display system logs

b) To search for text patterns in files

c) To create compressed archives

d) To change file permissions

Answer: b) To search for text patterns in files

Explanation: The grep command in Linux is used to search for text patterns in files.

Which command is used to delete a file in Linux?

a) rm

b) del

c) delete

d) remove

Answer: a) rm

Explanation: The rm command is used to delete a file in Linux.

How can you execute a previously executed command again in Linux?

a) Press Up arrow key

b) Press Down arrow key

c) Press Enter key

d) All of the above

Answer: d) All of the above

Explanation: You can execute a previously executed command again in Linux by pressing the Up arrow key to navigate to the desired command and then pressing Enter.

Which command is used to display disk usage statistics in Linux?

a) du

b) df

c) diskusage

d) diskstats

Answer: b) df

Explanation: The df command is used to display disk usage statistics in Linux.

What is the purpose of the chmod command in Linux?

a) To change file ownership

b) To change file permissions

c) To compress files

d) To rename files

Answer: b) To change file permissions

Explanation: The chmod command in Linux is used to change file permissions.

Which command is used to change the current directory in Linux?

a) cd

b) pwd

c) ls

d) mv

Answer: a) cd

Explanation: The cd command is used to change the current directory in Linux.

How can you search for a specific command in the command line history in Linux?

a) Using the grep command

b) Using the search command

c) Using the find command

d) Using the lookup command

Answer: a) Using the grep command

Explanation: You can search for a specific command in the command line history in Linux using the grep command.

Which option with the ls command is used to sort files by modification time, newest first?

a) -t

b) -l

c) -r

d) -h

Answer: a) -t

Explanation: The -t option with the ls command is used to sort files by modification time, newest first.

What is the purpose of the touch command in Linux?

a) To create an empty file

b) To move files and directories

c) To copy files and directories

d) To delete files and directories

Answer: a) To create an empty file

Explanation: The touch command in Linux is used to create an empty file.

How can you switch between user accounts in Linux?

a) Using the switchuser command

b) Using the su command

c) Using the changeuser command

d) Using the userchange command

Answer: b) Using the su command

Explanation: You can switch between user accounts in Linux using the su command.

Which command is used to display system uptime in Linux?

a) uptime

b) time

c) boottime

d) systemtime

Answer: a) uptime

Explanation: The uptime command is used to display system uptime in Linux.

What is the purpose of the pwd command in Linux?

a) To display disk usage statistics

b) To display system uptime

c) To display the current working directory

d) To display system logs

Answer: c) To display the current working directory

Explanation: The pwd command in Linux is used to display the current working directory.

Which command is used to copy files and directories in Linux?

a) cp

b) mv

c) rm

d) touch

Answer: a) cp

Explanation: The cp command is used to copy files and directories in Linux.

How can you access the manual page for a specific command in Linux?

a) Using the info command

b) Using the man command

c) Using the help command

d) Using the about command

Answer: b) Using the man command

Explanation: You can access the manual page for a specific command in Linux using the man command.

Which option with the ls command is used to display a long listing format?

a) -l

b) -a

c) -h

d) -t

Answer: a) -l

Explanation: The -l option with the ls command is used to display a long listing format.

What does the acronym GUI stand for in Linux?

a) Graphical Utility Interface

b) Global User Interaction

c) Graphical User Interface

d) General User Integration

Answer: c) Graphical User Interface

Explanation: GUI stands for Graphical User Interface in Linux.

How can you exit from the manual page viewer in Linux?

a) Press Q

b) Press Ctrl + C

c) Press Esc

d) All of the above

Answer: d) All of the above

Explanation: You can exit from the manual page viewer in Linux by pressing Q, Ctrl + C, or Esc.

Chapter 4: Vim Editor

The Vim editor, known for its power and efficiency, offers a multitude of features to enhance text editing tasks. In this chapter, we delve into the core functionalities of Vim, covering basic navigation, editing techniques, search and replacement, as well as copying and pasting operations.

Basic Navigation:

Navigating within a document is fundamental to efficient text editing. Vim provides numerous commands for moving the cursor through the text, including moving by characters, words, lines, and paragraphs. Understanding these navigation commands enables users to quickly traverse through documents and locate specific sections with ease.

Editing in Vim:

Vim offers a comprehensive set of editing commands for manipulating text. From inserting and deleting characters to cutting and pasting lines, Vim provides efficient shortcuts for common editing tasks. Additionally, Vim's modal editing paradigm allows seamless transitions between command mode and insert mode, facilitating fluid and intuitive text manipulation.

Search and Replacement:

Vim excels in facilitating search and replacement operations within documents. With powerful search commands and regular expression support, users can quickly locate specific patterns or occurrences of text. Furthermore, Vim offers robust replacement capabilities, allowing users to perform global replacements, selective replacements, and confirmation-based replacements to tailor the editing process to their needs.

Copying and Pasting:

Vim simplifies the process of copying and pasting text with intuitive commands. Users can effortlessly yank (copy) and put (paste) text within and across documents, leveraging Vim's registers to store and manipulate copied content. Additionally, Vim supports operations such as copying and pasting entire lines, blocks of text, and visual selections, further enhancing productivity in text editing workflows.

By mastering basic navigation, editing techniques, search and replacement functionalities, and copying and pasting operations in Vim, users can elevate their text editing prowess and streamline their workflow. Whether navigating large codebases, making precise edits to configuration files, or drafting lengthy documents, Vim empowers users to wield text editing capabilities with precision and efficiency, making it a indispensable tool for professionals and enthusiasts alike.

Practice Questions and Answers

How do you enter insert mode in Vim?

a) Press i

b) Press ESC

c) Press : followed by q

d) Press v

Answer: a) Press i

Explanation: Pressing i in command mode allows you to enter insert mode in Vim, where you can start typing and editing text.

Which command is used to save changes and exit Vim?

a) :q

b) :w

c) :q!

d) :wq

Answer: d) :wq

Explanation: The command :wq in command line mode is used to save changes and exit Vim.

What command is used to delete a single character under the cursor in Vim?

a) dd

b) x

c) dw

d) d$

Answer: b) x

Explanation: Pressing x deletes the character under the cursor in Vim.

How do you navigate to the end of a line in Vim?

a) Press $

b) Press gg

c) Press o

d) Press G

Answer: a) Press $

Explanation: Pressing $ in command mode moves the cursor to the end of the current line in Vim.

What command is used to copy a line in Vim?

a) yy

b) dd

c) cc

d) pp

Answer: a) yy

Explanation: Typing yy in command mode copies the current line in Vim.

How do you undo the last change in Vim?

a) :u

b) :undo

c) u

d) ctrl + z

Answer: c) u

Explanation: Pressing u in command mode undoes the last change in Vim.

Which command is used to search for a pattern in Vim?

a) /pattern

b) ?pattern

c) :search pattern

d) %pattern

Answer: a) /pattern

Explanation: Typing /pattern in command mode allows you to search forward for a pattern in Vim.

What does the command :%s/foo/bar/g do in Vim?

a) Searches for occurrences of "foo" and replaces them with "bar" globally

b) Searches for occurrences of "bar" and replaces them with "foo" globally

c) Deletes all lines containing "foo"

d) Deletes all lines containing "bar"

Answer: a) Searches for occurrences of "foo" and replaces them with "bar" globally

Explanation: The :%s/foo/bar/g command in command line mode searches for occurrences of "foo" and replaces them with "bar" globally in the document.

How do you move to the beginning of the document in Vim?

a) Press gg

b) Press G

c) Press 1G

d) Press o

Answer: a) Press gg

Explanation: Typing gg in command mode moves the cursor to the beginning of the document in Vim.

What command is used to move to the end of the document in Vim?

a) Press gg

b) Press G

c) Press 1G

d) Press $

Answer: b) Press G

Explanation: Typing G in command mode moves the cursor to the end of the document in Vim.

How do you delete a word in Vim?

a) Press d

b) Press dw

c) Press dd

d) Press x

Answer: b) Press dw

Explanation: Typing dw in command mode deletes the word under the cursor in Vim.

What does the command :set number do in Vim?

a) Turns on line numbering

b) Turns off line numbering

c) Sets the tab width to 8 spaces

d) Changes the font size

Answer: a) Turns on line numbering

Explanation: The :set number command in command line mode turns on line numbering in Vim.

How do you move to the next occurrence of a word in Vim?

a) Press n

b) Press N

c) Press *

d) Press #

Answer: a) Press n

Explanation: Typing n in command mode moves the cursor to the next occurrence of the word under the cursor in Vim.

What command is used to paste the contents of the clipboard in Vim?

a) :paste

b) :put

c) :p

d) :paste!

Answer: b) :put

Explanation: The :put command in command line mode is used to paste the contents of the clipboard in Vim.

How do you delete a line in Vim?

a) Press dd

b) Press d

c) Press x

d) Press yy

Answer: a) Press dd

Explanation: Typing dd in command mode deletes the current line in Vim.

What does the command :q! do in Vim?

a) Saves changes and exits Vim

b) Exits Vim without saving changes

c) Opens a new file in Vim

d) Creates a split window in Vim

Answer: b) Exits Vim without saving changes

Explanation: The :q! command in command line mode exits Vim without saving changes.

How do you select text in visual mode in Vim?

a) Press v

b) Press i

c) Press a

d) Press c

Answer: a) Press v

Explanation: Typing v in command mode enters visual mode in Vim, allowing you to select text.

What does the command :w do in Vim?

a) Saves changes and exits Vim

b) Exits Vim without saving changes

c) Saves changes to the file

d) Saves changes to a new file

Answer: c) Saves changes to the file

Explanation: The :w command in command line mode saves changes to the file in Vim.

How do you copy a line in Vim?

a) Press yy

b) Press cc

c) Press dd

d) Press pp

Answer: a) Press yy

Explanation: Typing yy in command mode copies the current line in Vim.

What does the command :e filename do in Vim?

a) Opens a new file

b) Edits an existing file

c) Exits Vim

d) Executes a shell command

Answer: b) Edits an existing file

Explanation: The :e filename command in command line mode opens an existing file for editing in Vim.

How do you move to the end of a line in Vim?

a) Press G

b) Press $

c) Press gg

d) Press A

Answer: b) Press $

Explanation: Typing $ in command mode moves the cursor to the end of the current line in Vim.

What command is used to paste the contents of the clipboard in Vim without auto-indenting?

a) :paste

b) :put

c) :p

d) :paste!

Answer: d) :paste!

Explanation: The :paste! command in command line mode is used to paste the contents of the clipboard in Vim without auto-indenting.

How do you move to the beginning of the document in Vim?

a) Press gg

b) Press G

c) Press 1G

d) Press o

Answer: a) Press gg

Explanation: Typing gg in command mode moves the cursor to the beginning of the document in Vim.

What command is used to search for a pattern in Vim backward?

a) ?pattern

b) /pattern

c) :search pattern

d) %pattern

Answer: a) ?pattern

Explanation: Typing ?pattern in command mode allows you to search backward for a pattern in Vim.

How do you move to the next occurrence of a word in Vim backward?

a) Press n

b) Press N

c) Press *

d) Press #

Answer: b) Press N

Explanation: Typing N in command mode moves the cursor to the next occurrence of the word under the cursor backward in Vim.

What command is used to delete the character under the cursor in Vim?

a) dd

b) x

c) dw

d) d$

Answer: b) x

Explanation: Pressing x deletes the character under the cursor in Vim.

What does the command :set number do in Vim?

a) Turns on line numbering

b) Turns off line numbering

c) Sets the tab width to 8 spaces

d) Changes the font size

Answer: a) Turns on line numbering

Explanation: The :set number command in command line mode turns on line numbering in Vim.

How do you undo the last change in Vim?

a) :u

b) :undo

c) u

d) ctrl + z

Answer: c) u

Explanation: Pressing u in command mode undoes the last change in Vim.

What does the command :%s/foo/bar/g do in Vim?

a) Searches for occurrences of "foo" and replaces them with "bar" globally

b) Searches for occurrences of "bar" and replaces them with "foo" globally

c) Deletes all lines containing "foo"

d) Deletes all lines containing "bar"

Answer: a) Searches for occurrences of "foo" and replaces them with "bar" globally

Explanation: The :%s/foo/bar/g command in command line mode searches for occurrences of "foo" and replaces them with "bar" globally in the document.

What command is used to paste the contents of the clipboard in Vim?

a) :paste

b) :put

c) :p

d) :paste!

Answer: b) :put

Explanation: The :put command in command line mode is used to paste the contents of the clipboard in Vim.

Chapter 5: Linux Files and Directories

Understanding the structure and organization of the Linux file system is essential for effective navigation and management of files and directories. In this chapter, we explore the Linux File System Hierarchy, learn techniques for navigating the file system, and delve into methods for exploring directory contents using various commands, including ls, ls -l, and ls -a.

Linux File System Hierarchy:

The Linux File System Hierarchy Standard (FHS) defines the structure and layout of directories in a Linux system. It organizes files and directories in a hierarchical manner, with each directory serving a specific purpose. Understanding the FHS is crucial for locating files, installing software, and maintaining system integrity.

Navigating the File System:

Navigating the Linux file system involves moving between directories to access and manage files. The cd (change directory) command is used to navigate the file system. By specifying the path to the desired directory, users can move to different locations within the file system effortlessly.

Exploring Directory Contents:

Exploring directory contents is facilitated by various commands, primarily the ls command. The ls command lists directory contents, providing users with valuable information about files and directories within the specified location. By appending different options to the ls command, such as -l (long listing format) and -a (include hidden files), users can customize the output to suit their needs.

cd Documents:

The cd Documents command is used to change the current working directory to the "Documents" directory. This command allows users to navigate directly to the "Documents" directory without specifying the full path. Once in the "Documents" directory, users can perform various operations, such as creating, modifying, and deleting files, within this specific directory context.

Explanation for cd Documents:

The cd (change directory) command is a fundamental command in Linux used to change the current working directory. When followed by a directory name, such as

"Documents," the cd command changes the current working directory to the specified directory.

In the context of the command "cd Documents," assuming "Documents" is a directory located within the current working directory or a subdirectory thereof, executing this command will change the current working directory to the "Documents" directory. This means that subsequent commands and operations will be performed within the "Documents" directory unless explicitly directed otherwise.

The cd command provides a convenient way to navigate through the file system hierarchy, allowing users to access and work with files and directories located in different locations. By using descriptive directory names, such as "Documents," users can easily identify and access specific directories within the file system.

Creating Directories:

The mkdir command is used to create directories in Linux. By specifying the name of the directory to be created, users can easily generate new directories within the file system. Creating directories is crucial for organizing files and facilitating efficient file management tasks.

mkdir school:

The mkdir school command creates a new directory named "school" within the current working directory. This command allows users to establish a directory named "school" without needing to specify the full path. Once created, the "school" directory can be utilized to store relevant files and subdirectories related to educational activities.

Finding Files:

The find command in Linux is a powerful tool for searching for files within the file system. With various options and parameters, users can customize the search criteria to locate specific files based on their attributes, such as name, size, type, and modification time. The find command is invaluable for locating files across the entire file system hierarchy.

Explanation for mkdir school:

The mkdir command in Linux is used to create directories. When followed by the name of the directory to be created, such as "school," the mkdir command generates a new directory with the specified name within the current working directory.

In the context of the command "mkdir school," executing this command creates a directory named "school" within the current directory. This means that a new directory named "school" will be created as a subdirectory of the directory from which the mkdir command is executed.

The mkdir command provides a straightforward method for users to create directories as needed, enabling efficient organization and structuring of files within the file system. By specifying meaningful directory names, such as "school," users can effectively categorize and manage their files according to specific contexts or purposes.

Explanation for find Command:

The find command in Linux is used to search for files and directories within the file system based on specified criteria. It traverses the directory hierarchy starting from the specified path (or the current directory if no path is provided) and recursively searches for files matching the given conditions.

Example usage of the find command:

bash

Copy code

```
find /home/user/documents -name "*.txt"
```

This command searches for files with the ".txt" extension within the "documents" directory located in the "/home/user" directory. The -name "*.txt" option specifies the search criteria, where "*.txt" denotes files with the ".txt" extension.

The find command offers various options and parameters to customize the search, allowing users to filter files based on attributes such as name, size, type, and modification time. It is a versatile tool for locating files and directories across the entire file system, aiding users in file management and organization tasks.

Locating Files:

The locate command is used to quickly find files by name within the Linux file system. It searches an index of all files and directories, providing fast and efficient results. The locate command is useful for locating files across the entire file system hierarchy.

Determining Command Locations:

Various commands, including which, whereis, and type, are used to determine the locations of executable files and commands within the Linux environment. These commands help users identify the paths of executable files associated with specific commands, aiding in troubleshooting and command usage.

Copying, Moving, and Deleting Files and Directories:

Copying, moving, and deleting files and directories are common operations in Linux file management. Commands such as cp (copy), mv (move), and rm (remove) are used to perform these tasks efficiently. Understanding how to use these commands is essential for effective file organization and management.

Explanation for each command:

locate Command:

The locate command in Linux is used to quickly find files by name. It searches an index of all files and directories stored on the system, providing fast results. For example, executing locate myfile.txt will search for and display the path(s) to the file named "myfile.txt" if it exists on the system.

which command:

The which command is used to determine the location of an executable file associated with a specified command. For example, which ls will display the path to the executable file for the ls command, indicating its location in the file system.

whereis command:

The whereis command is used to locate the binary, source, and manual page files for a specified command. For example, whereis python will display the paths to the binary executable, source code, and manual page files associated with the Python programming language.

type Command:

The type command is used to determine how a command name is interpreted by the shell. It displays information about the type of command, such as whether it is a shell built-in, an alias, a function, or an executable file. For example, type cp will indicate whether cp is a shell built-in command or an external executable file.

Copying, Moving, and Deleting Files and Directories:

The cp command is used to copy files and directories, the mv command is used to move files and directories, and the rm command is used to delete files and directories. These commands are essential for managing files and directories in Linux, allowing users to perform tasks such as creating backups, reorganizing file structures, and removing unwanted files.

Practice Questions and Answers

What command is used to create a new directory in Linux?

a) touch

b) mkdir

c) mkfile

d) newdir

Answer: b) mkdir

Explanation: The mkdir command is used to create a new directory in Linux.

How would you create a directory named "docs" in the current directory?

a) mkdir docs

b) create docs

c) newdir docs

d) touch docs

Answer: a) mkdir docs

Explanation: To create a directory named "docs" in the current directory, you would use the mkdir command followed by the directory name.

Which command is used to find files by name in Linux?

a) search

b) locate

c) find

d) grep

Answer: b) locate

Explanation: The locate command is used to find files by name in Linux.

How can you determine the location of an executable file associated with a specific command?

a) which

b) where

c) find

d) locate

Answer: a) which

Explanation: The which command is used to determine the location of an executable file associated with a specific command.

What does the command 'which ls' display?

a) The contents of the ls command

b) The location of the ls command's binary executable

c) The manual page for the ls command

d) The list of options available for the ls command

Answer: b) The location of the ls command's binary executable

Explanation: The 'which ls' command displays the location of the ls command's binary executable.

Which command is used to locate the binary, source, and manual page files for a specified command?

a) where

b) which

c) whereis

d) find

Answer: c) whereis

Explanation: The whereis command is used to locate the binary, source, and manual page files for a specified command.

How would you find all files with a .txt extension in the current directory and its subdirectories?

a) locate *.txt

b) find .txt

c) find . -name ".txt"

d) search .txt

Answer: c) find . -name "*.txt"

Explanation: The command 'find . -name "*.txt"' searches for all files with a .txt extension in the current directory and its subdirectories.

What command is used to determine how a command name is interpreted by the shell?

a) type

b) interpret

c) determine

d) check

Answer: a) type

Explanation: The type command is used to determine how a command name is interpreted by the shell.

How would you copy a file named "file1.txt" to a directory named "backup"?

a) cp file1.txt backup

b) mv file1.txt backup

c) copy file1.txt backup

d) cp file1.txt /backup

Answer: a) cp file1.txt backup

Explanation: The cp command is used to copy files in Linux. To copy "file1.txt" to the "backup" directory, you would use the command 'cp file1.txt backup'.

How do you move a file named "file2.txt" to a directory named "archive"?

a) move file2.txt archive

b) cp file2.txt archive

c) mv file2.txt archive

d) cut file2.txt archive

Answer: c) mv file2.txt archive

Explanation: The mv command is used to move files in Linux. To move "file2.txt" to the "archive" directory, you would use the command 'mv file2.txt archive'.

Which command is used to delete files in Linux?

a) delete

b) rm

c) del

d) remove

Answer: b) rm

Explanation: The rm command is used to delete files in Linux.

How would you delete a directory named "temp" and all its contents?

a) rm -r temp

b) del -rf temp

c) remove -r temp

d) rm -d temp

Answer: a) rm -r temp

Explanation: The '-r' option with the rm command is used to delete directories and their contents recursively in Linux. So, 'rm -r temp' would delete the directory "temp" and all its contents.

Which command is used to copy a directory and its contents recursively?

a) cp

b) mv

c) cp -r

d) mv -r

Answer: c) cp -r

Explanation: The 'cp -r' command is used to copy directories and their contents recursively in Linux.

How would you move a directory named "folder1" to another location?

a) move folder1 new_location

b) mv folder1 new_location

c) cp folder1 new_location

d) cut folder1 new_location

Answer: b) mv folder1 new_location

Explanation: The mv command is used to move directories in Linux. To move "folder1" to another location, you would use the command 'mv folder1 new_location'.

What does the command 'ls' do in Linux?

a) Lists all files and directories in the current directory

b) Lists only hidden files and directories

c) Lists files based on their modification time

d) Lists files in long format with detailed information

Answer: a) Lists all files and directories in the current directory

Explanation: The 'ls' command in Linux is used to list all files and directories in the current directory.

How would you list all files in the current directory, including hidden files?

a) ls -a

b) ls -l

c) ls -h

d) ls -s

Answer: a) ls -a

Explanation: The '-a' option with the ls command is used to list all files in the current directory, including hidden files.

What does the command 'ls -l' display?

a) Lists all files and directories in long format

b) Lists only directories in long format

c) Lists files based on their modification time

d) Lists files sorted by size

Answer: a) Lists all files and directories in long format

Explanation: The 'ls -l' command displays all files and directories in long format, providing detailed information such as permissions, owner, group, size, and modification time.

How would you list files and directories in the current directory in long format, including hidden files?

a) ls -lh

b) ls -al

c) ls -ll

d) ls -hl

Answer: b) ls -al

Explanation: The '-a' option with the ls command lists all files, and the '-l' option displays them in long format. Therefore, 'ls -al' lists files and directories in the current directory in long format, including hidden files.

What does the command 'ls -a' do in Linux?

a) Lists all files and directories in long format

b) Lists only hidden files and directories

c) Lists files based on their modification time

d) Lists files sorted by size

Answer: b) Lists only hidden files and directories

Explanation: The '-a' option with the ls command lists all files and directories, including hidden files and directories, in the current directory.

How would you list all files and directories in the current directory and its subdirectories?

a) ls -R

b) ls -r

c) ls -S

d) ls -A

Answer: a) ls -R

Explanation: The '-R' option with the ls command lists all files and directories recursively in the current directory and its subdirectories.

What does the command 'ls -R' display?

a) Lists all files and directories recursively

b) Lists files sorted by size

c) Lists only hidden files and directories

d) Lists files based on their modification time

Answer: a) Lists all files and directories recursively

Explanation: The 'ls -R' command displays all files and directories recursively, listing files and directories in the current directory and its subdirectories.

How would you list files in the current directory sorted by size, with the largest files listed first?

a) ls -s

b) ls -S

c) ls -lS

d) ls -sl

Answer: c) ls -lS

Explanation: The '-l' option with the ls command lists files in long format, and the '-S' option sorts them by size. Therefore, 'ls -lS' lists files in the current directory sorted by size, with the largest files listed first.

What does the command 'ls -h' do in Linux?

a) Lists files based on their modification time

b) Lists only hidden files and directories

c) Lists files in human-readable format

d) Lists files sorted by size

Answer: c) Lists files in human-readable format

Explanation: The '-h' option with the ls command displays file sizes in a human-readable format (e.g., KB, MB, GB).

How would you list files in the current directory with detailed information, including human-readable file sizes?

a) ls -lh

b) ls -lhS

c) ls -lhR

d) ls -lhT

Answer: a) ls -lh

Explanation: The '-l' option with the ls command displays detailed information, and the '-h' option displays file sizes in a human-readable format. Therefore, 'ls -lh' lists files in the current directory with detailed information, including human-readable file sizes.

What command is used to delete a directory named "folder" and all its contents in Linux?

a) delete folder

b) rm -r folder

c) rmdir folder

d) rm folder/*

Answer: b) rm -r folder

Explanation: The '-r' option with the rm command is used to delete directories and their contents recursively in Linux. Therefore, 'rm -r folder' deletes the directory "folder" and all its contents.

How would you copy a directory named "images" and its contents to a directory named "backup"?

a) cp -r images backup

b) mv -r images backup

c) cp -d images backup

d) mv -d images backup

Answer: a) cp -r images backup

Explanation: The 'cp -r' command is used to copy directories and their contents recursively in Linux. Therefore, 'cp -r images backup' copies the directory "images" and its contents to the directory "backup".

What command is used to move a directory named "docs" to another location in Linux?

a) move docs new_location

b) cp docs new_location

c) mv docs new_location

d) cut docs new_location

Answer: c) mv docs new_location

Explanation: The mv command is used to move directories in Linux. Therefore, 'mv docs new_location' moves the directory "docs" to another location.

How would you list files in the current directory sorted by modification time, with the most recently modified files listed first?

a) ls -t

b) ls -lt

c) ls -tL

d) ls -ltm

Answer: b) ls -lt

Explanation: The '-l' option with the ls command lists files in long format, and the '-t' option sorts them by modification time. Therefore, 'ls -lt' lists files in the current directory sorted by modification time, with the most recently modified files listed first.

What does the command 'ls -t' do in Linux?

a) Lists files sorted by modification time

b) Lists files sorted by size

c) Lists only hidden files and directories

d) Lists files in long format

Answer: a) Lists files sorted by modification time

Explanation: The 'ls -t' command lists files in the current directory sorted by modification time, with the most recently modified files listed first.

How would you list files in the current directory sorted by name in reverse order?

a) ls -r

b) ls -R

c) ls -s

d) ls -rS

Answer: d) ls -rS

Explanation: The '-r' option with the ls command lists files in reverse order, and the '-S' option sorts them by size. Therefore, 'ls -rS' lists files in the current directory sorted by name in reverse order.

Chapter 6: Managing Linux Users

In this chapter, we delve into the management of Linux users, including the administration of the root account, creating new users, modifying user attributes, and changing passwords. Understanding these aspects is essential for maintaining system security and user access control.

Root Account:

The root account, also known as the superuser or administrator account, possesses unrestricted access to the entire Linux system. It has the highest level of privileges, allowing it to execute commands, modify system files, and perform administrative tasks. Proper management of the root account is crucial to ensure system security and integrity.

The root account is the default administrative account in Linux systems. It is created during the installation process and has full control over the system. The root user can perform any operation on the system, including creating, modifying, and deleting files, installing software, and configuring system settings. However, it is important to exercise caution when using the root account, as any mistakes or malicious actions can have severe consequences for the system's stability and security.

Creating Users:

Creating new user accounts allows individuals to access the system with their own credentials and privileges. The useradd command is commonly used to create new users in Linux. When creating users, administrators can specify various attributes such as username, home directory, shell, and group membership.

To create a new user in Linux, the useradd command is used followed by the desired username. For example, to create a user named "john," you would use the command sudo useradd john. By default, useradd creates a new user with a home directory located at /home/username and assigns the /bin/bash shell. Additional options can be specified to customize user attributes during creation.

Modifying Users:

Modifying user attributes allows administrators to adjust user settings, such as changing the username, home directory, shell, or group membership. The usermod command is used to modify existing user accounts in Linux. Administrators can update user information as needed to accommodate changes in user roles or requirements.

To modify a user in Linux, the usermod command is employed followed by the desired modifications. For instance, to change the username of a user from "john" to "jdoe," you would use the command sudo usermod -l jdoe john. Similarly, other attributes such as the home directory (-d option), shell (-s option), and group membership (-g option) can be modified using appropriate usermod options.

Changing Passwords:

Changing user passwords is essential for maintaining account security and preventing unauthorized access. The passwd command enables users to change their passwords interactively. Administrators can also use the passwd command to change passwords for other users or enforce password policies.

To change a user's password in Linux, the passwd command is utilized followed by the username. For example, to change the password for the user "jdoe," you would use the command sudo passwd jdoe. The command prompts the user to enter their current password followed by the new password. Administrators can use the same command with appropriate privileges to change passwords for other users.

Managing Linux users is a critical aspect of system administration, ensuring proper access control and security measures are in place. By understanding the administration of the root account, creating and modifying users, and changing passwords, administrators can effectively manage user accounts and maintain the integrity of the Linux system.

Practice Questions and Answers

What is the root account in Linux?

a) A regular user account

b) An account with limited privileges

c) The administrator account with unrestricted access

d) A guest account

Answer: c) The administrator account with unrestricted access

Explanation: The root account in Linux is the superuser or administrator account with unrestricted access to the entire system. It possesses the highest level of privileges and can execute any command and modify system files. Other choices are incorrect because they do not accurately describe the root account.

Which command is commonly used to create new user accounts in Linux?

a) adduser

b) createuser

c) useradd

d) newuser

Answer: c) useradd

Explanation: The useradd command is commonly used to create new user accounts in Linux. It allows administrators to specify various attributes for the new user, such as the username, home directory, and shell. Other choices are not standard commands for creating user accounts in Linux.

How can you change the username of an existing user in Linux?

a) renameuser

b) changeuser

c) usermod -l

d) modifyuser

Answer: c) usermod -l

Explanation: The usermod command with the -l option is used to change the username of an existing user in Linux. For example, sudo usermod -l new_username old_username would change the username from old_username to new_username. Other choices are not valid commands for changing usernames in Linux.

What command is used to change a user's password in Linux?

a) setpassword

b) chpasswd

c) passwd

d) passchange

Answer: c) passwd

Explanation: The passwd command is used to change a user's password in Linux. It allows users to change their passwords interactively by prompting them to enter their current and new passwords. Other choices are not standard commands for changing passwords in Linux.

Which attribute can be modified using the usermod command in Linux?

a) User's full name

b) User's date of birth

c) User's group ID

d) User's email address

Answer: c) User's group ID

Explanation: The usermod command in Linux can be used to modify various attributes of a user account, including the user's group ID. The -g option with usermod is used to change the primary group of a user. Other choices are not attributes that can be directly modified using usermod.

What is the primary purpose of the root account in Linux?

a) To restrict access to system resources

b) To provide regular user privileges

c) To perform administrative tasks with unrestricted access

d) To serve as a guest account

Answer: c) To perform administrative tasks with unrestricted access

Explanation: The primary purpose of the root account in Linux is to perform administrative tasks with unrestricted access to the system. It is used to manage system resources, install software, configure settings, and perform other administrative functions. Other choices do not accurately describe the purpose of the root account.

How would you delete a user account in Linux?

a) rmuser

b) deleteuser

c) userdel

d) removeuser

Answer: c) userdel

Explanation: The userdel command is used to delete a user account in Linux. For example, sudo userdel username would delete the user account with the username specified. Other choices are not valid commands for deleting user accounts in Linux.

What command is used to lock a user account in Linux, preventing login?

a) lockuser

b) userlock

c) passwd -l

d) usermod -L

Answer: c) passwd -l

Explanation: The passwd command with the -l option is used to lock a user account in Linux, preventing login. For example, sudo passwd -l username would lock the user account specified by username. Other choices are not standard commands for locking user accounts in Linux.

Which file contains information about user accounts in Linux?

a) /etc/password

b) /etc/users

c) /etc/group

d) /etc/passwd

Answer: d) /etc/passwd

Explanation: The /etc/passwd file in Linux contains information about user accounts, including usernames, user IDs, group IDs, home directories, and shell paths. Other choices do not represent the file that contains user account information.

What does the useradd command do in Linux?

a) Adds a new user to the system

b) Deletes an existing user from the system

c) Modifies attributes of an existing user

d) Changes the password of an existing user

Answer: a) Adds a new user to the system

Explanation: The useradd command in Linux is used to add a new user to the system. It creates a new user account with default settings unless specified otherwise with additional options. Other choices represent different actions and commands in Linux user management.

How can you set an expiration date for a user account in Linux?

a) usermod -e

b) passwd -e

c) chage -E

d) userdel -e

Answer: a) usermod -e

Explanation: The usermod command with the -e option is used to set an expiration date for a user account in Linux. For example, sudo usermod -e 2024-12-31 username would set the expiration date for the user account specified by username to December 31, 2024. Other choices are not valid options for setting expiration dates for user accounts.

Which command is used to display information about user accounts in Linux?

a) userinfo

b) whoami

c) id

d) finger

Answer: d) finger

Explanation: The finger command is used to display information about user accounts in Linux, including username, login shell, home directory, and last login time. Other choices are not commands specifically designed to display user account information.

How can you assign a user to a supplementary group in Linux?

a) useradd -g

b) usermod -g

c) useradd -G

d) usermod -G

Answer: d) usermod -G

Explanation: The usermod command with the -G option is used to assign a user to a supplementary group in Linux. For example, sudo usermod -G groupname username would add the user specified by username to the supplementary group specified by groupname. Other choices are not valid options for assigning users to supplementary groups.

What is the default shell for the root account in most Linux distributions?

a) /bin/bash

b) /bin/sh

c) /usr/bin/zsh

d) /usr/bin/csh

Answer: a) /bin/bash

Explanation: The default shell for the root account in most Linux distributions is /bin/bash, the Bourne Again Shell. Other choices represent alternative shell options but are not the default shell for the root account.

How can you change the shell for an existing user in Linux?

a) usermod -s

b) chsh

c) passwd -s

d) chshell

Answer: a) usermod -s

Explanation: The usermod command with the -s option is used to change the shell for an existing user in Linux. For example, sudo usermod -s /bin/zsh username would change the shell for the user specified by username to /bin/zsh. Other choices are not valid options for changing the shell for users in Linux.

What is the purpose of the /etc/group file in Linux?

a) To store encrypted passwords for user accounts

b) To define groups and group memberships

c) To configure system-wide environmental variables

d) To log user login and logout times

Answer: b) To define groups and group memberships

Explanation: The /etc/group file in Linux is used to define groups and group memberships. It contains information about group names, group IDs, and the list of users belonging to each group. Other choices represent different purposes and files in Linux.

How can you force a user to change their password upon next login in Linux?

a) passwd -e

b) passwd -x

c) passwd -f

d) passwd -d

Answer: c) passwd -f

Explanation: The passwd command with the -f option is used to force a user to change their password upon next login in Linux. For example, sudo passwd -f username would prompt the user specified by username to change their password upon next login. Other choices are not valid options for forcing password changes upon next login.

Which command is used to add a user to a primary group in Linux?

a) useradd -g

b) usermod -g

c) useradd -G

d) usermod -G

Answer: a) useradd -g

Explanation: The useradd command with the -g option is used to add a user to a primary group in Linux. For example, sudo useradd -g groupname username would create a new user with the primary group specified by groupname. Other choices are not valid options for adding users to primary groups.

What does the command 'chage -l username' display in Linux?

a) The last login time of the user

b) The password aging information for the user

c) The groups the user belongs to

d) The expiration date of the user account

Answer: b) The password aging information for the user

Explanation: The 'chage -l username' command displays the password aging information for the user specified by username in Linux. It includes details such as the last password change date, password expiration date, and other password-related settings. Other choices represent different types of information not provided by the chage command.

How can you remove a user from a supplementary group in Linux?

a) userdel -G

b) usermod -G

c) userdel -g

d) usermod -g

Answer: b) usermod -G

Explanation: The usermod command with the -G option is used to remove a user from a supplementary group in Linux. For example, sudo usermod -G groupname username would remove the user specified by username from the supplementary group specified by groupname. Other choices are not valid options for removing users from supplementary groups.

What does the command 'id username' display in Linux?

a) The user's full name

b) The user's group memberships

c) The user's password aging information

d) The user's home directory

Answer: b) The user's group memberships

Explanation: The 'id username' command displays the group memberships of the user specified by username in Linux. It shows the user's primary group and any supplementary groups they belong to. Other choices represent different types of information not provided by the id command.

How can you unlock a user account in Linux, allowing login?

a) passwd -u

b) usermod -u

c) passwd -U

d) usermod -U

Answer: c) passwd -U

Explanation: The passwd command with the -U option is used to unlock a user account in Linux, allowing login. For example, sudo passwd -U username would unlock the user account specified by username. Other choices are not valid options for unlocking user accounts.

Which file stores encrypted passwords for user accounts in Linux?

a) /etc/passwd

b) /etc/shadow

c) /etc/group

d) /etc/passwords

Answer: b) /etc/shadow

Explanation: The /etc/shadow file in Linux stores encrypted passwords for user accounts. It contains information about user passwords, including the password hashes and password-related settings. Other choices do not represent the file that stores encrypted passwords.

How can you list all users in a Linux system?

a) cat /etc/passwd

b) getent passwd

c) ls -l /home

d) who

Answer: b) getent passwd

Explanation: The getent passwd command is used to list all users in a Linux system. It retrieves user account information from various sources, including the /etc/passwd file and network databases. Other choices do not accurately list all users in a Linux system.

What is the purpose of the /etc/shadow file in Linux?

a) To store user account information

b) To define groups and group memberships

c) To store encrypted passwords for user accounts

d) To log user login and logout times

Answer: c) To store encrypted passwords for user accounts

Explanation: The /etc/shadow file in Linux is used to store encrypted passwords for user accounts. It contains information about user passwords, including password hashes and password-related settings. Other choices represent different purposes and files in Linux.

How can you set the number of days after which a user's password expires in Linux?

a) chage -m

b) passwd -x

c) usermod -E

d) chage -M

Answer: d) chage -M

Explanation: The chage command with the -M option is used to set the maximum number of days after which a user's password expires in Linux. For example, sudo chage -M 90 username would set the password expiration interval to 90 days for the user specified by username. Other choices are not valid options for setting password expiration intervals.

How can you display the group memberships of a user in Linux?

a) groups username

b) id username

c) whoami

d) finger username

Answer: a) groups username

Explanation: The groups command followed by the username is used to display the group memberships of a user in Linux. For example, groups username would list all groups that the user specified by username belongs to. Other choices represent different commands and utilities in Linux.

What command is used to set a user's login shell in Linux?

a) chsh

b) passwd -s

c) usermod -s

d) chshell

Answer: a) chsh

Explanation: The chsh command is used to set a user's login shell in Linux. It prompts the user to enter the path to the desired shell. For example, sudo chsh username would allow the user specified by username to change their login shell. Other choices are not valid commands for setting login shells.

How can you display detailed information about a user account in Linux?

a) finger username

b) whoami

c) id username

d) userinfo username

Answer: a) finger username

Explanation: The finger command followed by the username is used to display detailed information about a user account in Linux, including the user's full name, login shell, home directory, and last login time. Other choices represent different commands and utilities in Linux.

What command is used to assign a user to a primary group in Linux?

a) useradd -g

b) usermod -g

c) useradd -G

d) usermod -G

Answer: a) useradd -g

Explanation: The useradd command with the -g option is used to assign a user to a primary group in Linux. For example, sudo useradd -g groupname username would create a new user with the primary group specified by groupname. Other choices are not valid options for assigning users to primary groups.

Chapter 7: Linux Groups

Understanding how groups function in Linux is essential for effective user management and access control within the system.

Creating Groups:

Groups in Linux allow for the organization and management of users with similar permissions or roles. The groupadd command is used to create new groups in Linux. When creating groups, administrators can specify various attributes such as the group name and group ID (GID).

To create a new group in Linux, the groupadd command is employed followed by the desired group name. For example, sudo groupadd mygroup would create a new group named "mygroup". By default, groupadd assigns the next available GID to the new group. Additional options can be specified to customize group attributes during creation.

Modifying Groups:

Modifying group attributes allows administrators to adjust group settings, such as changing the group name or GID. The groupmod command is used to modify existing groups in Linux. Administrators can update group information as needed to accommodate changes in group memberships or permissions.

To modify a group in Linux, the groupmod command is utilized followed by the desired modifications. For instance, to change the name of a group from "mygroup" to "newgroup," you would use the command sudo groupmod -n newgroup mygroup. Similarly, other attributes such as the GID (-g option) can be modified using appropriate groupmod options.

Administering Groups:

Administering groups involves managing group memberships, permissions, and access control within the system. The gpasswd command is commonly used to administer groups in Linux, allowing administrators to add or remove users from groups and set group passwords for added security.

The gpasswd command provides several options for administering groups in Linux. For example, sudo gpasswd -a username mygroup adds the user specified by username to the group "mygroup", while sudo gpasswd -r mygroup removes the group password for "mygroup". Administrators can use these commands to manage group memberships and enforce access control policies effectively.

ls Command:

The ls command is used to list directory contents in Linux, including files, directories, and symbolic links. When used with appropriate options, such as -l to display detailed information or -G to show group ownership, ls can provide insights into file and directory permissions and group associations.

By using the ls command with various options, administrators can inspect file and directory permissions and group ownership within the system. For example, ls -l displays detailed information about files and directories, including permissions, ownership, size, and modification time. Similarly, ls -G shows group ownership of files and directories in a human-readable format.

Understanding Linux groups and their administration is crucial for maintaining proper access control and security within the system. By mastering the creation, modification, and administration of groups, administrators can effectively manage user permissions and facilitate collaboration among users.

Practice Questions and Answers

What command is used to create a new group in Linux?

a) groupadd

b) addgroup

c) creategroup

d) newgroup

Answer: a) groupadd

Explanation: The groupadd command is used to create a new group in Linux. It creates a new group with the specified name.

Which command is used to add a user to a group in Linux?

a) useradd

b) usermod

c) groupadd

d) usergroup

Answer: b) usermod

Explanation: The usermod command is used to modify user accounts, including adding users to groups.

How can you change the name of an existing group in Linux?

a) groupmod -n

b) groupchange

c) grouprename

d) changegroup

Answer: a) groupmod -n

Explanation: The groupmod -n command is used to change the name of an existing group in Linux.

Which command is used to list all groups in Linux?

a) showgroups

b) listgroups

c) getent group

d) listall

Answer: c) getent group

Explanation: The getent group command lists all groups in Linux.

How can you remove a group in Linux?

a) groupdel

b) delgroup

c) removegroup

d) deletegroup

Answer: a) groupdel

Explanation: The groupdel command is used to remove a group in Linux.

What is the purpose of the gpasswd command in Linux?

a) To add a user to a group

b) To change the group password

c) To delete a group

d) To modify group permissions

Answer: b) To change the group password

Explanation: The gpasswd command is used to change the group password in Linux.

How can you display detailed information about a specific group in Linux?

a) groupinfo

b) showgroup

c) getent group

d) groupdetails

Answer: c) getent group

Explanation: The getent group command displays detailed information about a specific group in Linux.

Which file stores information about group memberships in Linux?

a) /etc/passwd

b) /etc/shadow

c) /etc/group

d) /etc/users

Answer: c) /etc/group

Explanation: The /etc/group file stores information about group memberships in Linux.

How can you add a user to a group using the gpasswd command?

a) gpasswd -a username groupname

b) gpasswd -u username groupname

c) gpasswd -g username groupname

d) gpasswd -add username groupname

Answer: a) gpasswd -a username groupname

Explanation: The gpasswd -a username groupname command is used to add a user to a group using the gpasswd command in Linux.

What is the purpose of the id command in Linux?

a) To display user information

b) To display group information

c) To display both user and group information

d) To change user or group settings

Answer: c) To display both user and group information

Explanation: The id command displays both user and group information in Linux.

How can you change the primary group of a user in Linux?

a) usermod -p

b) usermod -g

c) usermod -a

d) usermod -u

Answer: b) usermod -g

Explanation: The usermod -g command is used to change the primary group of a user in Linux.

Which command is used to assign multiple users to a group in Linux?

a) gpasswd -a

b) useradd -G

c) usermod -g

d) usermod -G

Answer: d) usermod -G

Explanation: The usermod -G command is used to assign multiple users to a group in Linux.

What is the purpose of the newgrp command in Linux?

a) To create a new group

b) To switch to a different group

c) To delete a group

d) To display group information

Answer: b) To switch to a different group

Explanation: The newgrp command is used to switch to a different group in Linux.

How can you display the members of a specific group in Linux?

a) showmembers

b) listmembers

c) getent group groupname

d) groupmembers

Answer: c) getent group groupname

Explanation: The getent group groupname command displays the members of a specific group in Linux.

Which command is used to change the group ownership of a file in Linux?

a) chgrp

b) chown

c) groupchown

d) changroup

Answer: a) chgrp

Explanation: The chgrp command is used to change the group ownership of a file in Linux.

What is the purpose of the groups command in Linux?

a) To display the groups a user belongs to

b) To display the users in a group

c) To list all groups in the system

d) To change group settings

Answer: a) To display the groups a user belongs to

Explanation: The groups command is used to display the groups a user belongs to in Linux.

How can you delete a user from a group using the gpasswd command?

a) gpasswd -r username groupname

b) gpasswd -d username groupname

c) gpasswd -remove username groupname

d) gpasswd -delete username groupname

Answer: b) gpasswd -d username groupname

Explanation: The gpasswd -d username groupname command is used to delete a user from a group using the gpasswd command in Linux.

Which command is used to change the group owner of a directory and its contents recursively?

a) chown -R

b) chgrp -R

c) chown -G

d) chgrp -G

Answer: b) chgrp -R

Explanation: The chgrp -R command is used to change the group owner of a directory and its contents recursively in Linux.

What is the default group name for a new user in Linux?

a) usergroup

b) users

c) default

d) primary

Answer: b) users

Explanation: The default group name for a new user in Linux is usually users.

How can you list the members of a specific group using the id command?

a) id -G groupname

b) id -g groupname

c) id -n groupname

d) id -m groupname

Answer: b) id -g groupname

Explanation: The id -g groupname command is used to list the members of a specific group using the id command in Linux.

Which command is used to change the group ID (GID) of an existing group?

a) groupmod -i

b) groupmod -g

c) groupmod -G

d) groupmod -n

Answer: b) groupmod -g

Explanation: The groupmod -g command is used to change the group ID (GID) of an existing group in Linux.

What is the purpose of the chown command in Linux?

a) To change the owner of a file or directory

b) To change the group ownership of a file or directory

c) To change both the owner and group ownership of a file or directory

d) To change file permissions

Answer: a) To change the owner of a file or directory

Explanation: The chown command is used to change the owner of a file or directory in Linux.

How can you display the primary group of a user in Linux?

a) id -p username

b) id -u username

c) id -G username

d) id -g username

Answer: d) id -g username

Explanation: The id -g username command is used to display the primary group of a user in Linux.

Which command is used to change the group ownership of a symbolic link in Linux?

a) chown

b) chgrp

c) linkchown

d) linkgrp

Answer: b) chgrp

Explanation: The chgrp command is used to change the group ownership of a symbolic link in Linux.

What is the purpose of the vigr command in Linux?

a) To edit the /etc/group file

b) To edit the /etc/passwd file

c) To edit the /etc/shadow file

d) To edit the /etc/gshadow file

Answer: a) To edit the /etc/group file

Explanation: The vigr command is used to edit the /etc/group file in Linux.

How can you remove a user from a group using the usermod command?

a) usermod -r username groupname

b) usermod -d username groupname

c) usermod -R username groupname

d) usermod -G username groupname

Answer: d) usermod -G username groupname

Explanation: The usermod -G username groupname command is used to remove a user from a group using the usermod command in Linux.

Which command is used to change the password of a group in Linux?

a) gpasswd -p

b) gpasswd -x

c) gpasswd -c

d) gpasswd -d

Answer: a) gpasswd -p

Explanation: The gpasswd -p command is used to change the password of a group in Linux.

What is the purpose of the grpck command in Linux?

a) To check the integrity of the /etc/group file

b) To check the integrity of the /etc/passwd file

c) To check the integrity of the /etc/shadow file

d) To check the integrity of the /etc/gshadow file

Answer: a) To check the integrity of the /etc/group file

Explanation: The grpck command is used to check the integrity of the /etc/group file in Linux.

How can you add a user to a group using the useradd command?

a) useradd -g groupname username

b) useradd -G groupname username

c) useradd -u groupname username

d) useradd -a groupname username

Answer: b) useradd -G groupname username

Explanation: The useradd -G groupname username command is used to add a user to a group using the useradd command in Linux.

Which command is used to display the members of a specific group using the members command?

a) members groupname

b) showmembers groupname

c) listmembers groupname

d) getent group groupname

Answer: a) members groupname

Explanation: The members groupname command is used to display the members of a specific group using the members command in Linux.

Chapter 8: Manage Software Applications

In this chapter, we delve into the management of software applications on Linux systems, focusing on two prominent tools: the RPM Package Manager and the Advanced Packaging Tool (APT). Understanding how to effectively manage software installations, updates, and removals is essential for maintaining a stable and secure system environment.

RPM Package Manager:

The RPM Package Manager is a command-line package management system used primarily by Red Hat-based Linux distributions. It provides a convenient way to install, query, verify, update, and remove software packages in the RPM format.

RPM packages are archives that contain software binaries, configuration files, and metadata necessary for installation. The rpm command is the primary tool for managing RPM packages. Administrators can use commands such as rpm -i to install packages, rpm -q to query package information, rpm -U to update packages, and rpm -e to remove packages.

Advanced Packaging Tool (APT):

APT is a package management system used primarily by Debian-based Linux distributions, including Ubuntu. It simplifies the process of installing, upgrading, and removing software packages and their dependencies.

APT relies on repositories—collections of software packages hosted online—to manage software installations. Administrators use commands such as apt-get and apt to interact with APT. For example, apt-get install installs packages, apt-get update refreshes the package lists from repositories, and apt-get remove removes packages. Additionally, APT provides features like dependency resolution and automatic updates, enhancing system management efficiency.

By mastering the RPM Package Manager and the Advanced Packaging Tool, administrators can effectively manage software applications on Linux systems, ensuring system stability, security, and productivity.

Practice Questions and Answers

What is the RPM Package Manager?

a) A command-line tool for managing software packages on Red Hat-based Linux distributions

b) A graphical package manager for Debian-based Linux distributions

c) A tool for creating compressed archives of files and directories

d) A system utility for managing hardware resources

Answer: a) A command-line tool for managing software packages on Red Hat-based Linux distributions

Which command is used to install an RPM package?

a) rpm -i

b) rpm -u

c) rpm -q

d) rpm -e

Answer: a) rpm -i

What does the command 'rpm -q package_name' do?

a) Installs the specified package

b) Queries information about the specified package

c) Updates the specified package

d) Removes the specified package

Answer: b) Queries information about the specified package

Which command is used to remove an RPM package?

a) rpm -i

b) rpm -u

c) rpm -q

d) rpm -e

Answer: d) rpm -e

What is the primary package management system used by Debian-based Linux distributions?

a) RPM Package Manager

b) Advanced Packaging Tool (APT)

c) YUM (Yellowdog Updater Modified)

d) DPKG (Debian Package)

Answer: b) Advanced Packaging Tool (APT)

Which command is used to install a package using APT?

a) apt-get remove

b) apt-get install

c) apt-get update

d) apt-get upgrade

Answer: b) apt-get install

How can you update the package lists from repositories using APT?

a) apt-get remove

b) apt-get install

c) apt-get update

d) apt-get upgrade

Answer: c) apt-get update

Which command is used to upgrade installed packages using APT?

a) apt-get remove

b) apt-get install

c) apt-get update

d) apt-get upgrade

Answer: d) apt-get upgrade

What is the purpose of the 'apt-cache search' command?

a) To search for installed packages

b) To search for available packages in repositories

c) To search for package updates

d) To search for package dependencies

Answer: b) To search for available packages in repositories

Which command is used to remove a package using APT?

a) apt-get remove

b) apt-get install

c) apt-get update

d) apt-get upgrade

Answer: a) apt-get remove

What is a repository in the context of package management?

a) A local directory containing software packages

b) A list of installed packages on a system

c) A collection of software packages hosted online

d) A configuration file for package managers

Answer: c) A collection of software packages hosted online

Which command is used to add a new repository in Debian-based Linux distributions?

a) add-apt-repository

b) apt-add-repository

c) add-repo

d) repo-add

Answer: b) apt-add-repository

What does the command 'dpkg -L package_name' do?

a) Installs the specified package

b) Lists files installed by the specified package

c) Queries information about the specified package

d) Removes the specified package

Answer: b) Lists files installed by the specified package

How can you force the removal of a package using APT?

a) apt-get remove --force

b) apt-get remove --force-yes

c) apt-get purge

d) apt-get autoremove

Answer: c) apt-get purge

What is the purpose of the 'apt-get autoremove' command?

a) Installs packages automatically

b) Removes unused dependencies

c) Upgrades installed packages

d) Purges configuration files of removed packages

Answer: b) Removes unused dependencies

Which command is used to show the dependencies of a package using APT?

a) apt-get dependencies

b) apt-cache depends

c) apt-get depends

d) apt-cache show

Answer: b) apt-cache depends

How can you downgrade a package using APT?

a) apt-get downgrade

b) apt-get install --old-version

c) apt-get update --downgrade

d) apt-get install --force-downgrade

Answer: b) apt-get install --old-version

What is the purpose of the 'yum repolist' command?

a) To list installed packages

b) To list available repositories

c) To list package dependencies

d) To list package updates

Answer: b) To list available repositories

Which command is used to install a package using YUM?

a) yum add

b) yum install

c) yum update

d) yum upgrade

Answer: b) yum install

How can you clean the YUM cache?

a) yum clean cache

b) yum clean

c) yum clean all

d) yum clean packages

Answer: c) yum clean all

What does the command 'rpm -V package_name' do?

a) Installs the specified package

b) Queries information about the specified package

c) Verifies the integrity of the specified package

d) Removes the specified package

Answer: c) Verifies the integrity of the specified package

How can you search for a package using the RPM Package Manager?

a) rpm -s package_name

b) rpm -q package_name

c) rpm -i package_name

d) rpm -f package_name

Answer: b) rpm -q package_name

Which command is used to verify all installed packages using the RPM Package Manager?

a) rpm -V

b) rpm -U

c) rpm -q

d) rpm -K

Answer: a) rpm -V

What is the purpose of the 'rpm -K' command?

a) Installs the specified package

b) Queries information about the specified package

c) Verifies the integrity of the specified package

d) Removes the specified package

Answer: c) Verifies the integrity of the specified package

How can you list all installed packages using the RPM Package Manager?

a) rpm -l

b) rpm -qa

c) rpm -i

d) rpm -U

Answer: b) rpm -qa

What does the command 'rpm -e package_name' do?

a) Installs the specified package

b) Queries information about the specified package

c) Updates the specified package

d) Removes the specified package

Answer: d) Removes the specified package

Which command is used to upgrade an RPM package?

a) rpm -i

b) rpm -u

c) rpm -q

d) rpm -e

Answer: b) rpm -u

How can you downgrade a package using the RPM Package Manager?

a) rpm -d package_name

b) rpm -U package_name

c) rpm -i --old-version package_name

d) rpm -U --old-package package_name

Answer: c) rpm -i --old-version package_name

What is the purpose of the 'yum list installed' command?

a) To list available packages

b) To list installed packages

c) To list package updates

d) To list package dependencies

Answer: b) To list installed packages

Which command is used to reinstall a package using YUM?

a) yum install

b) yum reinstall

c) yum update

d) yum upgrade

Answer: b) yum reinstall

Chapter 9: Managing Processes

Understanding how to list, background, foreground, and terminate processes is essential for effective system administration and resource management.

Listing Running Processes:

To view information about processes currently running on the system, administrators can use commands like ps, top, or htop. These commands display details such as process IDs (PIDs), resource usage, execution status, and parent-child relationships.

The ps command (Process Status) is a versatile tool for listing processes. Options like -e (all processes), -f (full-format listing), and -aux (detailed listing with user and CPU information) provide flexibility in output.

top and htop are interactive tools that offer real-time monitoring of processes. They display CPU and memory usage, update dynamically, and allow users to sort and manipulate process data.

Background Processes:

Running processes in the background allows users to execute multiple tasks simultaneously without blocking the command line interface. To launch a process in the background, append an ampersand & to the command.

Background processes do not occupy the foreground terminal, allowing users to continue working without interruption.

Background processes can be managed using job control commands like bg (move a stopped or background job to the background), fg (bring a background job to the foreground), and jobs (list active jobs).

Backgrounding Foreground Processes:

Users can background foreground processes by suspending them with Ctrl + Z and then using the bg command to resume execution in the background.

Suspending a foreground process with Ctrl + Z halts its execution and returns control to the terminal.

By issuing the bg command after suspending a process, users instruct the system to resume execution in the background.

Killing Processes:

Terminating unwanted or malfunctioning processes is crucial for system stability and resource optimization. The kill command is used to send signals to processes, allowing users to gracefully terminate or forcefully kill them.

The kill command sends signals to processes specified by their PID. The default signal, SIGTERM (signal 15), requests termination, while SIGKILL (signal 9) forcibly terminates a process.

Process IDs can be obtained from commands like ps, top, or pgrep, and signals can be sent using their corresponding PID.

Understanding how to effectively manage processes enables administrators to maintain system performance, troubleshoot issues, and optimize resource utilization in Linux environments.

Practice Questions and Answers

How can you list all running processes in Linux?

a) ps -a

b) ps -e

c) ps -r

d) ps -l

Answer: b) ps -e

Explanation: The ps -e command lists all running processes in Linux. The -e option stands for "everyone" and displays information about all processes on the system.

Which command displays real-time information about processes?

a) ps

b) top

c) kill

d) bg

Answer: b) top

Explanation: The top command displays real-time information about processes, including CPU and memory usage, process IDs, and more.

How can you run a process in the background?

a) Append the & symbol to the command

b) Use the bg command

c) Press Ctrl + Z

d) Use the fg command

Answer: a) Append the & symbol to the command

Explanation: Appending the & symbol to a command runs it in the background, allowing you to continue using the terminal while the process executes.

What does pressing Ctrl + Z do in Linux?

a) Kills the foreground process

b) Suspends the foreground process

c) Moves the foreground process to the background

d) Restarts the foreground process

Answer: b) Suspends the foreground process

Explanation: Pressing Ctrl + Z suspends the foreground process, allowing you to resume it later or move it to the background.

Which command is used to bring a background process to the foreground?

a) fg

b) bg

c) kill

d) ps

Answer: a) fg

Explanation: The fg command is used to bring a background process to the foreground, allowing you to interact with it directly.

How can you terminate a process gracefully?

a) kill -9 PID

b) kill -15 PID

c) kill -1 PID

d) kill -6 PID

Answer: b) kill -15 PID

Explanation: Using kill -15 PID sends a SIGTERM signal to the process, allowing it to terminate gracefully and perform cleanup tasks before exiting.

Which command is used to send signals to processes?

a) ps

b) top

c) kill

d) bg

Answer: c) kill

Explanation: The kill command is used to send signals to processes, allowing you to control their behavior.

What does the -9 option in the kill command signify?

a) Suspend the process

b) Terminate the process forcefully

c) Bring the process to the foreground

d) Terminate the process gracefully

Answer: b) Terminate the process forcefully

Explanation: Using kill -9 PID sends a SIGKILL signal to the process, forcibly terminating it without allowing it to perform cleanup tasks.

How can you terminate multiple processes with the same name?

a) killall process_name

b) kill -a process_name

c) kill -all process_name

d) kill -f process_name

Answer: a) killall process_name

Explanation: The killall command is used to terminate multiple processes with the same name.

What does the ps -l command do?

a) Lists all processes

b) Lists processes in long format

c) Lists processes in real-time

d) Lists processes in user format

Answer: b) Lists processes in long format

Explanation: The ps -l command lists processes in long format, providing detailed information about each process.

How can you kill a process by its process ID (PID)?

a) kill -p PID

b) kill -ID PID

c) kill -9 PID

d) kill -PID PID

Answer: c) kill -9 PID

Explanation: The kill -9 PID command sends a SIGKILL signal to the process with the specified PID, forcibly terminating it.

Which command displays the process ID (PID) of a running process?

a) pid

b) ps

c) top

d) pgrep

Answer: d) pgrep

Explanation: The pgrep command is used to search for processes by name and display their PIDs.

How can you view the parent process ID (PPID) of a process?

a) ps -p PID

b) ps -f PID

c) ps -l PID

d) ps -ppid PID

Answer: c) ps -l PID

Explanation: The ps -l PID command displays detailed information about a specific process, including its parent process ID (PPID).

Which command displays the CPU and memory usage of processes in real-time?

a) ps

b) top

c) kill

d) bg

Answer: b) top

Explanation: The top command displays real-time information about processes, including CPU and memory usage.

How can you display all processes owned by a specific user?

a) ps -u username

b) ps -user username

c) ps -l username

d) ps -f username

Answer: a) ps -u username

Explanation: The ps -u username command displays all processes owned by the specified user.

What does the bg command do?

a) Brings a background process to the foreground

b) Suspends a foreground process

c) Terminates a process

d) Lists background processes

Answer: d) Lists background processes

Explanation: The bg command lists background processes and their job IDs.

How can you display a hierarchical tree of processes?

a) ps -h

b) ps -t

c) pstree

d) top -h

Answer: c) pstree

Explanation: The pstree command displays a hierarchical tree of processes, showing parent-child relationships.

Which command is used to change the priority of a process?

a) nice

b) priority

c) renice

d) top -p

Answer: c) renice

Explanation: The renice command is used to change the priority of a running process.

How can you suspend a running process temporarily?

a) kill -STOP PID

b) kill -SUSPEND PID

c) kill -PAUSE PID

d) kill -SIGSTOP PID

Answer: d) kill -SIGSTOP PID

Explanation: The kill -SIGSTOP PID command suspends a running process temporarily.

What does the fg command do?

a) Lists background processes

b) Brings a background process to the foreground

c) Suspends a foreground process

d) Terminates a process

Answer: b) Brings a background process to the foreground

Explanation: The fg command brings a background process to the foreground, allowing you to interact with it directly.

How can you terminate all processes belonging to a specific user?

a) killall -u username

b) kill -u username

c) kill -all username

d) kill -f username

Answer: a) killall -u username

Explanation: The killall -u username command terminates all processes belonging to the specified user.

Which signal is sent by default when using the kill command without specifying a signal number?

a) SIGKILL

b) SIGTERM

c) SIGSTOP

d) SIGCONT

Answer: b) SIGTERM

Explanation: The kill command sends a SIGTERM signal by default, allowing the process to terminate gracefully.

What does the -l option in the kill command do?

a) Lists available signals

b) Lists all running processes

c) Lists background processes

d) Lists suspended processes

Answer: a) Lists available signals

Explanation: The kill -l command lists available signals that can be sent to processes.

How can you terminate a process without sending a signal?

a) kill -q PID

b) kill -n PID

c) kill -p PID

d) kill -o PID

Answer: d) kill -o PID

Explanation: The kill -o PID command checks if a process exists without sending any signal.

What is the purpose of the nice command?

a) Sets the priority of a process

b) Suspends a process

c) Lists all processes

d) Lists background processes

Answer: a) Sets the priority of a process

Explanation: The nice command is used to adjust the priority of a process, influencing its scheduling in the CPU.

How can you kill all processes with a specific name?

a) killall process_name

b) kill -n process_name

c) kill -all process_name

d) kill -f process_name

Answer: a) killall process_name

Explanation: The killall process_name command terminates all processes with the specified name.

What does the pkill command do?

a) Sends signals to processes by name

b) Lists processes by name

c) Suspends processes by name

d) Terminates processes by name

Answer: a) Sends signals to processes by name

Explanation: The pkill command sends signals to processes based on their name.

How can you display the command line arguments of a running process?

a) ps -c PID

b) ps -f PID

c) ps -l PID

d) ps -a PID

Answer: a) ps -c PID

Explanation: The ps -c PID command displays the command line arguments of a running process.

What does the kill -HUP PID command do?

a) Suspends the process

b) Terminates the process gracefully

c) Terminates the process forcefully

d) Reloads the configuration of the process

Answer: d) Reloads the configuration of the process

Explanation: The kill -HUP PID command sends a SIGHUP signal to the process, instructing it to reload its configuration.

How can you prioritize a process to use less CPU resources?

a) renice -n 19 PID

b) renice -n 0 PID

c) renice -n -19 PID

d) renice -n 10 PID

Answer: c) renice -n -19 PID

Explanation: The renice -n -19 PID command prioritizes a process to use fewer CPU resources by setting its priority to the lowest value.

Chapter 10: Networking in Linux

Understanding how to configure network settings, troubleshoot connectivity issues, and utilize networking tools is essential for system administrators and users alike.

Network Configuration:

Configuring network settings involves tasks such as assigning IP addresses, configuring interfaces, setting up routing tables, and managing network services. Tools like ifconfig, ip, and configuration files in /etc/network directory are commonly used for network configuration.

The ifconfig command is used to configure network interfaces, assign IP addresses, and manage network paramcters.

The ip command is a more modern replacement for ifconfig, offering advanced functionality for configuring network interfaces, routing, and more.

Configuration files in the /etc/network directory, such as interfaces and resolv.conf, provide a way to persistently configure network settings across system reboots.

Network Troubleshooting:

Troubleshooting network issues involves diagnosing connectivity problems, identifying misconfigurations, and resolving network-related errors. Tools like ping, traceroute, netstat, and tcpdump are commonly used for network troubleshooting.

The ping command is used to test network connectivity by sending ICMP echo request packets to a specified host and waiting for replies.

traceroute is a tool used to trace the route taken by packets from the source to the destination, showing the IP addresses of intermediate hops.

netstat provides information about network connections, routing tables, interface statistics, and more.

tcpdump is a packet analyzer that captures and displays network packets, allowing users to inspect network traffic for troubleshooting purposes.

Network Services:

Linux supports various network services such as DNS (Domain Name System), DHCP (Dynamic Host Configuration Protocol), FTP (File Transfer Protocol), SSH (Secure Shell), and more. Configuring and managing these services is essential for providing network functionality to users and applications.

DNS translates domain names to IP addresses and vice versa, facilitating communication between networked devices.

DHCP dynamically assigns IP addresses and network configuration parameters to devices on a network, simplifying network administration.

FTP enables file transfer between client and server systems over a network, providing a convenient way to share files.

SSH provides secure remote access to systems over a network, allowing users to log in and execute commands securely.

Understanding networking concepts and tools empowers Linux users and administrators to configure, troubleshoot, and manage network resources effectively, ensuring reliable connectivity and communication across systems.

Chapter 11: Permissions

Understanding how permissions work is crucial for maintaining security and controlling access to files and directories.

Changing File Ownership:

Changing file ownership involves transferring ownership of files and directories from one user to another. The chown command is used for changing ownership, allowing administrators to assign ownership to specific users and groups.

The chown command is used to change the owner and group owner of files and directories in Linux.

Ownership can be specified using user and group names or numerical user and group IDs (UID and GID).

Administrators can recursively change ownership for entire directory trees using the -R option.

Permissions Basics:

File and directory permissions define who can read, write, and execute files or directories. Permissions are represented by symbolic notation (e.g., rwx) or octal notation (e.g., 755). Understanding permission basics is essential for controlling access to sensitive data and system resources.

Permissions are divided into three categories: owner, group, and others.

Each category has three types of permissions: read (r), write (w), and execute (x).

Permissions can be viewed using commands like ls -l, where they are represented as a series of symbols indicating read (r), write (w), and execute (x) permissions.

Modifying File Permissions:

Modifying file permissions involves changing the access rights of files and directories to grant or restrict access to users and groups. The chmod command is used for modifying permissions, allowing administrators to set permissions explicitly using symbolic or octal notation.

The chmod command is used to modify permissions of files and directories in Linux.

Permissions can be modified using symbolic notation (e.g., u+r to add read permission for the owner) or octal notation (e.g., 755 to set permissions to read, write, and execute for the owner, and read and execute for group and others).

Administrators can use the chmod command with the -R option to recursively change permissions for entire directory trees.

Understanding file and directory permissions is crucial for maintaining security and controlling access to sensitive data and system resources in Linux environments. Effective permission management ensures that only authorized users can access and modify files and directories, enhancing system security and integrity.

Practice Questions and Answers

What command is used to display IP address information of network interfaces in Linux?

a) ipconfig

b) ifconfig

c) netstat

d) route

Answer: b) ifconfig

Explanation: The ifconfig command is used to display IP address information of network interfaces in Linux.

Which command is used to view the routing table in Linux?

a) netstat -r

b) ifconfig

c) route

d) ip route

Answer: d) ip route

Explanation: The ip route command is used to view the routing table in Linux.

How can you assign an IP address to a network interface temporarily?

a) Edit the /etc/network/interfaces file

b) Use the ifconfig command followed by the interface name and the IP address

c) Use the ipconfig command followed by the interface name and the IP address

d) Use the route command followed by the interface name and the IP address

Answer: b) Use the ifconfig command followed by the interface name and the IP address

Explanation: The ifconfig command followed by the interface name and the IP address can be used to assign an IP address to a network interface temporarily.

What command is used to test network connectivity by sending ICMP echo requests?

a) traceroute

b) netstat

c) ping

d) telnet

Answer: c) ping

Explanation: The ping command is used to test network connectivity by sending ICMP echo requests.

Which command is used to display active network connections and listening ports?

a) netstat

b) ifconfig

c) route

d) ping

Answer: a) netstat

Explanation: The netstat command is used to display active network connections and listening ports.

How can you view the MAC (Media Access Control) address of a network interface in Linux?

a) Use the ifconfig command

b) Use the netstat command

c) Use the route command

d) Use the ipconfig command

Answer: a) Use the ifconfig command

Explanation: The ifconfig command displays the MAC address of a network interface in Linux.

What command is used to perform a DNS lookup in Linux?

a) nslookup

b) dig

c) host

d) ping

Answer: a) nslookup

Explanation: The nslookup command is used to perform a DNS lookup in Linux.

How can you set up a static IP address in Linux permanently?

a) Edit the /etc/network/interfaces file

b) Use the ifconfig command

c) Use the ipconfig command

d) Use the route command

Answer: a) Edit the /etc/network/interfaces file

Explanation: Editing the /etc/network/interfaces file allows you to set up a static IP address in Linux permanently.

Which command is used to display detailed information about network interfaces, including IP addresses and MAC addresses?

a) ifconfig

b) netstat

c) ipconfig

d) route

Answer: a) ifconfig

Explanation: The ifconfig command is used to display detailed information about network interfaces, including IP addresses and MAC addresses.

How can you release and renew DHCP leases for network interfaces in Linux?

a) Use the dhclient command

b) Use the ifdown and ifup commands

c) Use the ipconfig /release and ipconfig /renew commands

d) Use the route command

Answer: a) Use the dhclient command

Explanation: The dhclient command is used to release and renew DHCP leases for network interfaces in Linux.

What is the purpose of the route command in Linux?

a) To display the routing table

b) To configure network interfaces

c) To test network connectivity

d) To perform a DNS lookup

Answer: a) To display the routing table

Explanation: The route command in Linux is used to display the routing table.

Which command is used to trace the route taken by packets from the source to the destination?

a) trace

b) traceroute

c) route

d) netstat

Answer: b) traceroute

Explanation: The traceroute command is used to trace the route taken by packets from the source to the destination.

How can you view the network interfaces configured on a Linux system?

a) Use the ifconfig command

b) Use the netstat command

c) Use the route command

d) Use the ipconfig command

Answer: a) Use the ifconfig command

Explanation: The ifconfig command is used to view the network interfaces configured on a Linux system.

What is the purpose of the dig command in Linux?

a) To perform a DNS lookup

b) To display network interface information

c) To test network connectivity

d) To display routing information

Answer: a) To perform a DNS lookup

Explanation: The dig command in Linux is used to perform a DNS lookup.

How can you view the IP address assigned to a specific network interface in Linux?

a) Use the ipconfig command

b) Use the ifconfig command followed by the interface name

c) Use the netstat command

d) Use the route command

Answer: b) Use the ifconfig command followed by the interface name

Explanation: Using the ifconfig command followed by the interface name allows you to view the IP address assigned to a specific network interface in Linux.

Which command is used to display the hostname of a Linux system?

a) host

b) dig

c) nslookup

d) hostname

Answer: d) hostname

Explanation: The hostname command is used to display the hostname of a Linux system.

How can you test network connectivity to a specific host and port in Linux?

a) Use the ping command

b) Use the netstat command

c) Use the telnet command

d) Use the ifconfig command

Answer: c) Use the telnet command

Explanation: The telnet command is used to test network connectivity to a specific host and port in Linux.

What is the purpose of the host command in Linux?

a) To perform a DNS lookup

b) To display network interface information

c) To test network connectivity

d) To display routing information

Answer: a) To perform a DNS lookup

Explanation: The host command in Linux is used to perform a DNS lookup.

How can you view the DNS servers configured on a Linux system?

a) Use the ifconfig command

b) Use the resolv.conf file

c) Use the netstat command

d) Use the route command

Answer: b) Use the resolv.conf file

Explanation: DNS servers configured on a Linux system can be viewed by inspecting the resolv.conf file.

Which command is used to display the routing table in Linux in a more detailed format?

a) netstat -r

b) route

c) ip route

d) ifconfig

Answer: c) ip route

Explanation: The ip route command is used to display the routing table in Linux in a more detailed format.

How can you configure a network interface to automatically obtain an IP address from a DHCP server?

a) Use the ifconfig command

b) Edit the /etc/network/interfaces file

c) Use the ipconfig command

d) Use the dhclient command

Answer: d) Use the dhclient command

Explanation: The dhclient command is used to configure a network interface to automatically obtain an IP address from a DHCP server.

What does the arp command do in Linux?

a) Displays the ARP cache

b) Tests network connectivity

c) Displays detailed network interface information

d) Performs a DNS lookup

Answer: a) Displays the ARP cache

Explanation: The arp command in Linux is used to display the ARP (Address Resolution Protocol) cache.

How can you view the DNS domain name configured on a Linux system?

a) Use the dig command

b) Use the nslookup command

c) Use the hostname command

d) Use the resolv.conf file

Answer: d) Use the resolv.conf file

Explanation: The DNS domain name configured on a Linux system can be viewed by inspecting the resolv.conf file.

What is the purpose of the netstat command in Linux?

a) To display network interface information

b) To perform a DNS lookup

c) To test network connectivity

d) To display active network connections

Answer: d) To display active network connections

Explanation: The netstat command in Linux is used to display active network connections.

How can you view the status of network interfaces in Linux?

a) Use the ifstatus command

b) Use the ipstatus command

c) Use the ifconfig command

d) Use the netstat command

Answer: c) Use the ifconfig command

Explanation: The ifconfig command is used to view the status of network interfaces in Linux.

What does the telnet command do in Linux?

a) Tests network connectivity

b) Performs a DNS lookup

c) Displays detailed network interface information

d) Allows you to log in to remote systems

Answer: d) Allows you to log in to remote systems

Explanation: The telnet command in Linux allows you to log in to remote systems.

How can you view the default gateway configured on a Linux system?

a) Use the ifconfig command

b) Use the route command

c) Use the resolv.conf file

d) Use the netstat command

Answer: b) Use the route command

Explanation: The default gateway configured on a Linux system can be viewed using the route command.

What is the purpose of the nslookup command in Linux?

a) To perform a DNS lookup

b) To display network interface information

c) To test network connectivity

d) To display routing information

Answer: a) To perform a DNS lookup

Explanation: The nslookup command in Linux is used to perform a DNS lookup.

How can you view the network configuration of all network interfaces in Linux?

a) Use the ifconfig -a command

b) Use the netstat -a command

c) Use the route -a command

d) Use the ipconfig -a command

Answer: a) Use the ifconfig -a command

Explanation: The ifconfig -a command is used to view the network configuration of all network interfaces in Linux.

What does the ifup command do in Linux?

a) Brings a network interface up

b) Brings a network interface down

c) Displays network interface information

d) Tests network connectivity

Answer: a) Brings a network interface up

Explanation: The ifup command in Linux brings a network interface up, enabling network connectivity.

Chapter 12: Hardware Management

In this chapter, we explore various aspects of hardware management in Linux, covering topics such as Interrupt Request (IRQ), I/O Ports, Kernel Modules, CPU Information, System Information, USB Devices, Hard Disks Configuration, and Creating a New Partition. Understanding hardware management is essential for system administrators and users to effectively manage and configure hardware resources in Linux environments.

Interrupt Request (IRQ):

Interrupt Requests (IRQs) are signals sent to the CPU to notify it of an event that requires its attention. In Linux, IRQs are used to manage hardware interrupts such as those generated by peripherals like keyboards, mice, and network cards. Understanding IRQs is crucial for troubleshooting hardware-related issues and optimizing system performance.

I/O Ports:

Input/Output (I/O) Ports are hardware interfaces used for communication between the CPU and peripheral devices. In Linux, I/O ports are managed by the kernel and device drivers, allowing applications to interact with hardware devices efficiently. Knowledge of I/O ports is important for configuring and troubleshooting hardware peripherals in Linux systems.

Kernel Modules:

Kernel Modules are dynamically loadable code segments that extend the functionality of the Linux kernel. They allow device drivers and other essential components to be loaded and unloaded from memory as needed, providing flexibility and modularity to the kernel. Understanding kernel modules is essential for managing hardware devices, adding new features, and customizing the Linux kernel.

Loading Kernel Modules:

Loading Kernel Modules involves dynamically adding new functionality to the Linux kernel at runtime. This process allows device drivers and other kernel components to be loaded into memory, enabling support for hardware devices and additional features. Knowing how to load kernel modules is crucial for adding support for new hardware and extending the capabilities of the Linux kernel.

Removing Kernel Modules:

Removing Kernel Modules involves unloading dynamically loaded code segments from the Linux kernel to free up memory and resources. This process allows unused device drivers and kernel components to be unloaded, improving system stability and performance. Understanding how to remove kernel modules is important for managing system resources and troubleshooting kernel-related issues.

Getting CPU Info:

Getting CPU Information involves retrieving detailed information about the Central Processing Unit (CPU) installed in a Linux system. This information includes details such as CPU model, architecture, speed, cache size, and more. Understanding CPU information is essential for optimizing system performance, identifying hardware limitations, and troubleshooting CPU-related issues.

Getting System Information:

Getting System Information involves gathering comprehensive details about the hardware and software configuration of a Linux system. This information includes data such as the kernel version, memory size, disk partitions, installed packages, and more. Understanding system information is crucial for system administrators to monitor system health, diagnose problems, and plan system upgrades.

USB Devices:

Universal Serial Bus (USB) Devices are widely used for connecting peripherals such as keyboards, mice, printers, storage devices, and more to Linux systems. Managing USB devices involves detecting, configuring, and controlling their operation in Linux environments. Knowledge of USB device management is important for ensuring compatibility, troubleshooting connectivity issues, and optimizing performance.

Hard Disks Configuration:

Hard Disks Configuration involves managing storage devices such as hard disks and Solid-State Drives (SSDs) in Linux systems. This includes tasks such as partitioning disks, formatting file systems, mounting and unmounting partitions, and managing disk quotas. Understanding hard disk configuration is essential for data storage, retrieval, and management in Linux environments.

Creating a New Partition:

Creating a New Partition involves dividing a storage device into multiple logical sections called partitions. In Linux, partitions are used to organize data, install operating systems, and allocate storage space efficiently. Knowledge of partitioning is important for managing disk storage, optimizing file system performance, and supporting multi-boot configurations.

Understanding hardware management in Linux is essential for effectively utilizing and optimizing hardware resources in diverse computing environments. From managing device interrupts and kernel modules to configuring storage devices and USB peripherals, a comprehensive understanding of hardware management enables system administrators and users to maintain stable, reliable, and efficient Linux systems.

Practice Questions and Answers

What is the purpose of an Interrupt Request (IRQ) in hardware management?

a) To handle system crashes

b) To notify the CPU of an event that requires its attention

c) To manage memory allocation

d) To regulate power consumption

Answer: b) To notify the CPU of an event that requires its attention

Explanation: Interrupt Requests (IRQs) are signals sent to the CPU to notify it of an event that requires its attention, such as hardware interrupts from peripherals.

Which command is used to view the list of IRQs assigned to hardware devices in Linux?

a) lsirq

b) irqview

c) cat /proc/interrupts

d) showirq

Answer: c) cat /proc/interrupts

Explanation: The cat /proc/interrupts command is used to view the list of IRQs assigned to hardware devices in Linux.

What do I/O Ports represent in hardware management?

a) Physical ports for connecting input/output devices

b) Internal storage locations for device drivers

c) Virtual addresses for accessing hardware registers

d) Memory locations for storing temporary data

Answer: c) Virtual addresses for accessing hardware registers

Explanation: I/O Ports represent virtual addresses used for accessing hardware registers in hardware management.

How can you list the currently loaded kernel modules in Linux?

a) listmodules

b) showkernel

c) lsmod

d) modulelist

Answer: c) lsmod

Explanation: The lsmod command is used to list the currently loaded kernel modules in Linux.

What command is used to load a kernel module into memory in Linux?

a) addmod

b) insmod

c) loadmodule

d) kernelload

Answer: b) insmod

Explanation: The insmod command is used to load a kernel module into memory in Linux.

How can you unload a kernel module from memory in Linux?

a) removemod

b) delmod

c) rmmod

d) unloadmodule

Answer: c) rmmod

Explanation: The rmmod command is used to unload a kernel module from memory in Linux.

What command provides detailed information about the CPU in Linux?

a) cpuinfo

b) cpudetails

c) cat /proc/cpuinfo

d) showcpu

Answer: c) cat /proc/cpuinfo

Explanation: The cat /proc/cpuinfo command provides detailed information about the CPU in Linux.

How can you determine the number of CPU cores in a Linux system?

a) cat /proc/cores

b) ls /proc/cpu

c) cat /proc/cpuinfo | grep "cores"

d) corecount

Answer: c) cat /proc/cpuinfo | grep "cores"

Explanation: The cat /proc/cpuinfo | grep "cores" command can be used to determine the number of CPU cores in a Linux system.

Which command is used to view system information, including hardware details, in Linux?

a) hwinfo

b) systeminfo

c) cat /proc/systeminfo

d) uname -a

Answer: d) uname -a

Explanation: The uname -a command is used to view system information, including hardware details, in Linux.

How can you list USB devices connected to a Linux system?

a) lsusb

b) usbinfo

c) cat /proc/usb

d) usblist

Answer: a) lsusb

Explanation: The lsusb command is used to list USB devices connected to a Linux system.

What command displays detailed information about hard disks and partitions in Linux?

a) diskinfo

b) hddetails

c) fdisk -l

d) diskutil

Answer: c) fdisk -l

Explanation: The fdisk -l command displays detailed information about hard disks and partitions in Linux.

How can you create a new partition on a disk in Linux?

a) createpart

b) partition

c) mkpart

d) newpart

Answer: c) mkpart

Explanation: The mkpart command is used to create a new partition on a disk in Linux.

Which file contains information about loaded kernel modules in Linux?

a) /etc/modules

b) /proc/modules

c) /var/modules

d) /sys/modules

Answer: b) /proc/modules

Explanation: Information about loaded kernel modules in Linux can be found in the /proc/modules file.

How can you view the list of available I/O ports in Linux?

a) lsio

b) cat /proc/ioports

c) ioportlist

d) showports

Answer: b) cat /proc/ioports

Explanation: The cat /proc/ioports command can be used to view the list of available I/O ports in Linux.

What command is used to display information about USB controllers and devices in Linux?

a) usbinfo

b) lsusb

c) cat /proc/usbinfo

d) listusb

Answer: b) lsusb

Explanation: The lsusb command is used to display information about USB controllers and devices in Linux.

How can you view information about the currently loaded kernel modules and their dependencies in Linux?

a) lsmod

b) modinfo

c) depmod

d) moduleinfo

Answer: a) lsmod

Explanation: The lsmod command is used to view information about the currently loaded kernel modules and their dependencies in Linux.

What command provides detailed information about disk partitions in Linux?

a) partitioninfo

b) diskdetails

c) fdisk -l

d) parted -l

Answer: c) fdisk -l

Explanation: The fdisk -l command provides detailed information about disk partitions in Linux.

How can you load a kernel module automatically during system boot in Linux?

a) Add it to /etc/modules.conf

b) Add it to /etc/kernel.modules

c) Add it to /etc/modules

d) Add it to /etc/modprobe.d

Answer: c) Add it to /etc/modules

Explanation: Adding the kernel module to the /etc/modules file ensures that it is loaded automatically during system boot in Linux.

Which command is used to display information about CPU architecture in Linux?

a) cpuarch

b) cat /proc/cpuinfo

c) cpudetail

d) showcpuarch

Answer: b) cat /proc/cpuinfo

Explanation: The cat /proc/cpuinfo command displays information about CPU architecture in Linux.

How can you view the status of kernel modules in Linux?

a) Use the lsmod command

b) Use the modinfo command

c) Use the cat /proc/modules command

d) Use the showmodules command

Answer: a) Use the lsmod command

Explanation: The lsmod command is used to view the status of kernel modules in Linux.

What is the purpose of the /proc/interrupts file in Linux?

a) It contains information about IRQs assigned to hardware devices

b) It lists the available I/O ports

c) It provides detailed CPU information

d) It displays information about USB devices

Answer: a) It contains information about IRQs assigned to hardware devices

Explanation: The /proc/interrupts file in Linux contains information about IRQs assigned to hardware devices.

How can you display detailed information about USB devices connected to a Linux system?

a) cat /proc/usb

b) listusb

c) usbinfo

d) lsusb -v

Answer: d) lsusb -v

Explanation: The lsusb -v command is used to display detailed information about USB devices connected to a Linux system.

What command is used to view the status of kernel modules, including their dependencies?

a) lsmod

b) modinfo

c) depmod

d) moduleinfo

Answer: a) lsmod

Explanation: The lsmod command is used to view the status of kernel modules, including their dependencies, in Linux.

How can you display the currently assigned IRQs in Linux?

a) cat /proc/irqs

b) lsirq

c) showirq

d) cat /proc/interrupts

Answer: d) cat /proc/interrupts

Explanation: The cat /proc/interrupts command displays the currently assigned IRQs in Linux.

What is the purpose of the modprobe command in Linux?

a) To display information about kernel modules

b) To load and unload kernel modules

c) To list USB devices

d) To configure I/O ports

Answer: b) To load and unload kernel modules

Explanation: The modprobe command in Linux is used to load and unload kernel modules.

How can you view detailed information about a specific kernel module in Linux?

a) lsmod

b) modinfo

c) cat /proc/modules

d) moduleinfo

Answer: b) modinfo

Explanation: The modinfo command is used to view detailed information about a specific kernel module in Linux.

Which file contains information about currently loaded kernel modules in Linux?

a) /etc/modules

b) /proc/modules

c) /var/modules

d) /sys/modules

Answer: b) /proc/modules

Explanation: Information about currently loaded kernel modules in Linux can be found in the /proc/modules file.

What command is used to display information about CPU architecture and features in Linux?

a) cpuarch

b) cat /proc/cpuinfo

c) cpudetail

d) showcpuarch

Answer: b) cat /proc/cpuinfo

Explanation: The cat /proc/cpuinfo command displays information about CPU architecture and features in Linux.

How can you display the list of USB controllers and their associated devices in Linux?

a) usbinfo

b) lsusb -v

c) cat /proc/usb

d) showusb

Answer: b) lsusb -v

Explanation: The lsusb -v command displays the list of USB controllers and their associated devices in Linux.

What is the purpose of the depmod command in Linux?

a) To display information about kernel modules

b) To load and unload kernel modules

c) To list USB devices

d) To generate module dependency information

Answer: d) To generate module dependency information

Explanation: The depmod command in Linux is used to generate module dependency information, which is required for proper module loading and unloading.

Chapter 13: Booting Linux

In this chapter, we delve into the process of booting Linux systems, covering important topics such as GRUB version 1, Configuring Grub Legacy, GRUB Version 2, and Linux Runlevels. Understanding the boot process is essential for system administrators and users to troubleshoot boot-related issues, configure boot loaders, and manage system startup behavior effectively.

GRUB version 1:

GRUB (Grand Unified Bootloader) version 1, also known as GRUB Legacy, is a widely used boot loader for Linux systems. It provides a menu-based interface for selecting operating systems and kernel options during system startup. Understanding GRUB version 1 is crucial for configuring and managing the boot process on Linux systems that use this bootloader.

Configuring Grub Legacy:

Configuring Grub Legacy involves customizing its settings and options to suit specific system requirements. This includes configuring the bootloader menu, setting default boot options, and managing kernel parameters. Knowledge of configuring Grub Legacy is essential for system administrators to optimize system boot performance and troubleshoot boot-related issues.

GRUB Version 2:

GRUB Version 2 is the successor to GRUB Legacy, offering enhanced features and capabilities for booting Linux and other operating systems. It provides improved support for modern hardware and file systems, as well as advanced configuration options. Understanding GRUB Version 2 is important for managing the boot process on newer Linux systems and ensuring compatibility with modern hardware.

Linux Runlevels:

Linux Runlevels are predefined operating states or system configurations that determine which services and processes are started or stopped during system boot. They range from single-user mode (Runlevel 1) to fully multi-user mode with graphical interface (Runlevel 5), along with other intermediate states. Understanding Linux Runlevels is essential for managing system startup behavior and performing troubleshooting tasks.

Mastering the booting process in Linux empowers system administrators and users to effectively configure boot loaders, troubleshoot boot issues, and optimize system startup performance. From understanding the intricacies of GRUB bootloaders to managing

Linux runlevels, this chapter equips readers with the knowledge and skills necessary to ensure smooth and efficient system booting.

Practice Question and Answers

What is the purpose of a boot loader in Linux?

a) To load the operating system into memory during system startup

b) To manage user authentication

c) To configure network settings

d) To manage disk partitions

Answer: a) To load the operating system into memory during system startup

Explanation: A boot loader is responsible for loading the operating system into memory and initiating the boot process during system startup.

Which boot loader is commonly used in Linux systems?

a) GRUB

b) LILO

c) NTLDR

d) BOOTMGR

Answer: a) GRUB

Explanation: GRUB (Grand Unified Bootloader) is a commonly used boot loader in Linux systems.

What does GRUB stand for?

a) Grand Unified Bootloader

b) Graphical User Boot Loader

c) General Utility Boot Loader

d) Global Resource Usage Boot

Answer: a) Grand Unified Bootloader

Explanation: GRUB stands for Grand Unified Bootloader.

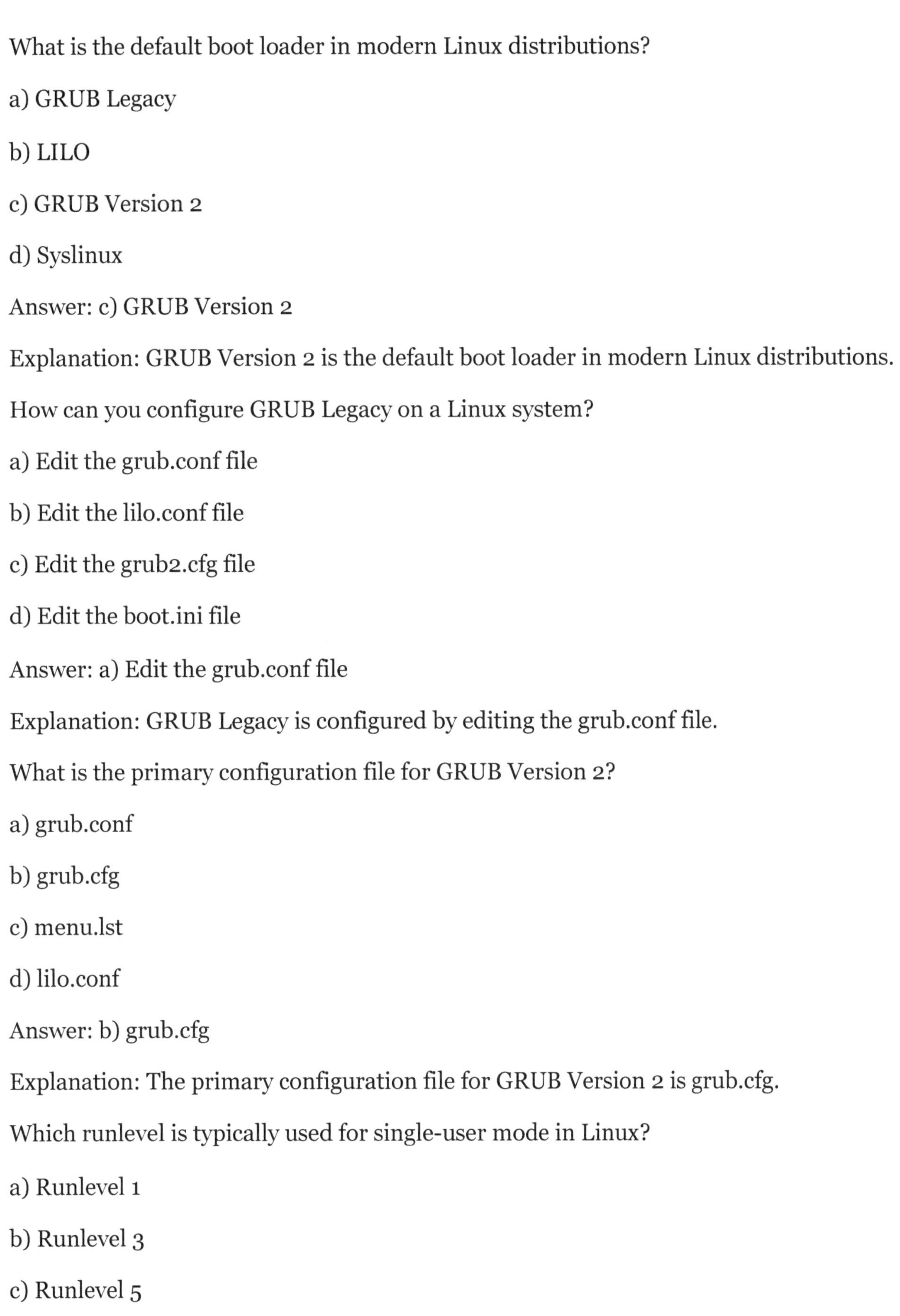

What is the default boot loader in modern Linux distributions?

a) GRUB Legacy

b) LILO

c) GRUB Version 2

d) Syslinux

Answer: c) GRUB Version 2

Explanation: GRUB Version 2 is the default boot loader in modern Linux distributions.

How can you configure GRUB Legacy on a Linux system?

a) Edit the grub.conf file

b) Edit the lilo.conf file

c) Edit the grub2.cfg file

d) Edit the boot.ini file

Answer: a) Edit the grub.conf file

Explanation: GRUB Legacy is configured by editing the grub.conf file.

What is the primary configuration file for GRUB Version 2?

a) grub.conf

b) grub.cfg

c) menu.lst

d) lilo.conf

Answer: b) grub.cfg

Explanation: The primary configuration file for GRUB Version 2 is grub.cfg.

Which runlevel is typically used for single-user mode in Linux?

a) Runlevel 1

b) Runlevel 3

c) Runlevel 5

d) Runlevel 7

Answer: a) Runlevel 1

Explanation: Runlevel 1 is typically used for single-user mode in Linux.

How can you change the default runlevel in Linux?

a) Edit the /etc/rc.conf file

b) Edit the /etc/inittab file

c) Use the runlevel command

d) Use the update-rc.d command

Answer: b) Edit the /etc/inittab file

Explanation: The default runlevel in Linux can be changed by editing the /etc/inittab file.

Which command is used to display the current runlevel in Linux?

a) runlevel

b) showlevel

c) currentlevel

d) cat /etc/runlevel

Answer: a) runlevel

Explanation: The runlevel command is used to display the current runlevel in Linux.

What is the purpose of runlevel 5 in Linux?

a) Single-user mode

b) Multi-user mode with networking

c) Multi-user mode with a graphical interface

d) Emergency mode

Answer: c) Multi-user mode with a graphical interface

Explanation: Runlevel 5 in Linux is typically used for multi-user mode with a graphical interface.

How can you specify kernel parameters during boot with GRUB?

a) Edit the grub.conf file

b) Edit the /etc/inittab file

c) Use the init command

d) Use the bootparam command

Answer: a) Edit the grub.conf file

Explanation: Kernel parameters during boot with GRUB are specified by editing the grub.conf file.

What is the purpose of the initrd image in Linux?

a) To load the initial RAM disk

b) To load the kernel into memory

c) To configure network settings

d) To manage user authentication

Answer: a) To load the initial RAM disk

Explanation: The initrd image in Linux is used to load the initial RAM disk during the boot process.

Which command is used to install GRUB on the Master Boot Record (MBR) of a disk?

a) grub-install

b) install-grub

c) setup-grub

d) update-grub

Answer: a) grub-install

Explanation: The grub-install command is used to install GRUB on the Master Boot Record (MBR) of a disk.

How can you boot into single-user mode using GRUB?

a) Append "single" to the kernel command line

b) Append "runlevel=1" to the kernel command line

c) Append "init=/bin/bash" to the kernel command line

d) Append "emergency" to the kernel command line

Answer: c) Append "init=/bin/bash" to the kernel command line

Explanation: You can boot into single-user mode using GRUB by appending "init=/bin/bash" to the kernel command line.

What is the purpose of the runlevel command in Linux?

a) To change the default runlevel

b) To display the current runlevel

c) To list available runlevels

d) To restart the system

Answer: b) To display the current runlevel

Explanation: The runlevel command is used to display the current runlevel in Linux.

How can you reboot a Linux system using the init command?

a) init 0

b) init 6

c) init 3

d) init 5

Answer: b) init 6

Explanation: The init 6 command reboots a Linux system using the init command.

Which command is used to shut down a Linux system immediately?

a) shutdown now

b) shutdown -h now

c) poweroff

d) halt

Answer: c) poweroff

Explanation: The poweroff command is used to shut down a Linux system immediately.

What is the purpose of the /etc/inittab file in Linux?

a) To configure kernel parameters

b) To specify runlevel configurations

c) To configure network settings

d) To manage user accounts

Answer: b) To specify runlevel configurations

Explanation: The /etc/inittab file in Linux is used to specify runlevel configurations.

How can you switch between runlevels in Linux?

a) Use the runlevel command

b) Use the init command

c) Use the chroot command

d) Use the boot command

Answer: b) Use the init command

Explanation: You can switch between runlevels in Linux using the init command.

What does the "rd" option in kernel parameters stand for in GRUB?

a) Run Directory

b) Root Disk

c) RAM Disk

d) Run Daemon

Answer: c) RAM Disk

Explanation: In GRUB, the "rd" option in kernel parameters stands for RAM Disk.

Which runlevel is used for system maintenance and troubleshooting in Linux?

a) Runlevel 1

b) Runlevel 3

c) Runlevel 5

d) Runlevel S

Answer: a) Runlevel 1

Explanation: Runlevel 1 in Linux is used for system maintenance and troubleshooting.

How can you specify a different init binary during boot with GRUB?

a) Use the initrd command

b) Use the kernel command

c) Use the init=/path/to/init option

d) Use the ramdisk command

Answer: c) Use the init=/path/to/init option

Explanation: You can specify a different init binary during boot with GRUB by using the init=/path/to/init option.

What does the "ro" option in kernel parameters stand for in GRUB?

a) Read Only

b) Root On

c) Run Once

d) Root Off

Answer: a) Read Only

Explanation: In GRUB, the "ro" option in kernel parameters stands for Read Only.

How can you specify a different runlevel during boot with GRUB?

a) Use the runlevel command

b) Use the init command

c) Use the single command

d) Use the runlevel= option

Answer: d) Use the runlevel= option

Explanation: You can specify a different runlevel during boot with GRUB by using the runlevel= option.

What is the purpose of the init process in Linux?

a) To manage user accounts

b) To initialize system resources

c) To configure network settings

d) To start and stop system services

Answer: b) To initialize system resources

Explanation: The init process in Linux is responsible for initializing system resources during boot.

How can you access GRUB's command-line interface during boot?

a) Press F2

b) Press Esc

c) Press Enter

d) Press Tab

Answer: b) Press Esc

Explanation: You can access GRUB's command-line interface during boot by pressing Esc.

Which runlevel is used for emergency mode in Linux?

a) Runlevel 1

b) Runlevel 3

c) Runlevel 5

d) Runlevel S

Answer: d) Runlevel S

Explanation: Runlevel S in Linux is used for emergency mode.

How can you specify a different root filesystem during boot with GRUB?

a) Use the rootfs command

b) Use the root= option

c) Use the bootroot command

d) Use the filesystem command

Answer: b) Use the root= option

Explanation: You can specify a different root filesystem during boot with GRUB by using the root= option.

What does the "rw" option in kernel parameters stand for in GRUB?

a) Read Write

b) Root Write

c) Run Without

d) RAM Write

Answer: a) Read Write

Explanation: In GRUB, the "rw" option in kernel parameters stands for Read Write.

How can you specify a different initial RAM disk (initrd) image during boot with GRUB?

a) Use the initrd= option

b) Use the ramdisk= option

c) Use the ramfs= option

d) Use the initramfs= option

Answer: a) Use the initrd= option

Explanation: You can specify a different initial RAM disk (initrd) image during boot with GRUB by using the initrd= option.

Conclusion

In this book, we have explored the fundamentals of Linux, covering a wide range of topics essential for understanding and mastering the Linux operating system. From basic commands and file system navigation to advanced concepts like managing users, groups, and permissions, each chapter has provided comprehensive coverage of key Linux concepts and practices.

Throughout the book, readers have engaged with practice questions and answers designed to reinforce their understanding and test their knowledge. These practice questions have allowed readers to apply what they've learned in a practical context, preparing them for real-world scenarios and certification exams.

As we conclude this book, it is important to emphasize the importance of continued learning and hands-on practice. Linux is a powerful and versatile operating system with a vast ecosystem of tools and technologies. By continuing to explore and experiment with Linux, readers can deepen their understanding and proficiency, enabling them to tackle increasingly complex challenges and contribute to the ever-evolving world of technology.

Whether you are a beginner looking to build a strong foundation in Linux or an experienced user seeking to expand your skills, this book has provided valuable insights and resources to support your journey. Remember, the world of Linux is vast and ever-changing, and there is always something new to discover and learn.

Thank you for joining us on this journey through Linux, and we wish you continued success in your exploration of this remarkable operating system.

Happy Linuxing!